DO YOU KNOW WHY . . .

. . . a mortgage is literally a death pledge?

. . . guns have girls' names?

. . . salt is related to soldier?

You're about to find out . . .

The
Etymologicon

A Circular Stroll
Through the
Hidden Connections
of the English
Language

MARK FORSYTH

BERKLEY
New York

BERKLEY
An imprint of Penguin Random House LLC
penguinrandomhouse.com

ISBN: 9780425260791

The Berkley trade paperback edition of this title has been cataloged by the Library of Congress
LC record available at https://lccn.loc.gov/2012533123

Icon Books Ltd., UK hardcover edition / November 2011
Berkley trade paperback edition / October 2012

Printed in the United States of America

Cover design by Danielle Abbiate
Book design by Tiffany Estreicher

For John Goldsmith,
with thanks.

The author would like to thank everybody involved with
the production of this book, but especially Jane Seeber and
Andrea Coleman for their advice, suggestions, corrections,
clarifications and other gentle upbraidings.

. . . they who are so exact for the letter shall be
dealt with by the **Lexicon**, and the **Etymologicon**
too if they please . . .

—JOHN MILTON

This book is the papery child of the Inky Fool blog, which was started in 2009. Though most of the material is new, some of it has been adapted from its computerised parent. The blog is available at http://blog.inkyfool.com, which is a part of the grander whole www.inkyfool.com.

CONTENTS

Contents

Contents

Contents

PREFACE

(or that which is said—*fatus*—before)

Occasionally people make the mistake of asking me where a word comes from. They never make this mistake twice. I am naturally a stern and silent fellow; even forbidding. But there's something about etymology and where words come from that overcomes my inbuilt taciturnity. A chap once asked me where the word *biscuit* came from. He was eating one at the time and had been struck by curiosity.

I explained to him that a biscuit is cooked twice, or in French *bi-cuit*, and he thanked me for that. So I added that the *bi* in biscuit is the same *bi* that you get in *bicycle* and *bisexual*, to which he nodded. And then, just because it occurred to me, I told him that the word bisexual wasn't invented until the 1890s and that it was coined by a psychiatrist called Richard von Krafft-Ebing and did he know that Ebing also invented the word *masochism*?

He told me firmly that he didn't.

Did he know about Mr. Masoch, after whom masochism was named? He was a novelist and . . .

The fellow told me that he didn't know about Mr. Masoch, that he didn't want to know about Mr. Masoch, and that his one ambition in life was to eat his biscuit in peace.

But it was too late. The metaphorical floodgates had opened and the horse had bolted. You see there are a lot of other words named after novelists, like Kafkaesque and Retifism . . .

It was at this point that he made a dash for the door, but I was too quick for him. My blood was up and there was always something more to say. There always is, you know. There's always an extra connection, another link that joins two words that most of mankind quite blithely believe to be separate, which is why that fellow didn't escape until a couple of hours later when he managed to climb out of the window while I was drawing a diagram to explain what the name Philip has to do with a hippopotamus.

It was after an incident such as this that my friends and family decided something must be done. They gathered for a confabulation and, having established that secure psychiatric care was beyond their means, they turned in despair to the publishing industry, which has a long history of picking up where social work leaves off.

So, a publisher was found somewhere near the Caledonian Road and a plan was hatched. I would start with a single word and then connect it to another word and then to another word and so on and so forth until I was exhausted and could do no more.

A book would therefore have a twofold benefit. First, it would rid me of my demons and perhaps save some innocent conversationalist from my clutches. Second, unlike me, a book could be left snugly on the bedside table or beside the lavatory: opened at will and *closed* at will.

So a book it was, which set me thinking . . .

The
Etymologicon

THE ETYMOLOGICON

A Turn-up for the Books

This is a book. The glorious insanities of the English language mean that you can do all sorts of odd and demeaning things to a book. You can cook it. You can bring a criminal to it, or, if the criminal refuses to be brought, you can throw it at him. You may even take a leaf out of it, the price of lavatory paper being what it is. But there is one thing that you can never do to a book like this. Try as and how you might, you cannot turn up for it. Because *a turn-up for the books* has nothing, directly, to do with the ink-glue-and-paper affair that this is (that is, unless you're terribly modern and using a Kindle or somesuch). It's *a turn-up for the bookmakers*.

Any child who sees the bookmaker's facing the bookshop across the High Street will draw the seemingly logical conclusion. And a bookmaker was, once, simply somebody who stuck books together. Indeed, the term *bookmaker* used to be used to describe the kind of writer who just pumps out one shelf-filler after another with no regard for the exhaustion of the reading public. Thomas More observed in 1533 that "of newe booke makers there are now moe then ynough." Luckily for the book trade, More was beheaded a couple of years later.

The modern sense of the bookmaker as a man who takes bets originated on the racecourses of Victorian Britain. The bookmaker would accept bets from anyone who wanted to lay them, and note them all down in a big betting book. Meanwhile, a turn-up was just a happy chance. A dictionary of slang from 1873 thoughtfully gives us this definition:

> **Turn up** an unexpected slice of luck. Among sporting men bookmakers are said to have a turn up when an unbacked horse wins.

So, which horses are unbacked? Those with the best (i.e., longest) odds. Almost nobody backs a horse at a thousand to one.

This may seem a rather counterintuitive answer. Odds of a thousand to one are enough to tempt even a saint to stake his halo, but that's because saints don't know anything about gambling and horseflesh. Thousand-to-one shots never, ever come in. Every experienced gambler knows that a race is very often won by the favourite, which will of course have short odds. Indeed, punters want to back a horse that's so far ahead of the field he merely needs to be shooed over the line. Such a horse is a *shoo-in*.

So you pick the favourite, and you back it. Nobody but a fool backs a horse that's unlikely to win. So when such an unfancied nag romps over the finish line, it's a turn-up for the books, because the bookies won't have to pay out.

Not that the bookmakers need much luck. They always win. There will always be many more bankrupt gamblers than bookies. You're much better off in a zero-sum game, where the players pool their money and the winner takes all. Pooling your money began in France, and has nothing whatsoever to do with swimming pools, and a lot to do with chickens and genetics.

A Game of Chicken

Gambling in medieval France was a simple business. All you needed were some friends, a pot, and a chicken. In fact, you didn't need friends—you could do this with your enemies—but the pot and the chicken were essential.

First, each person puts an equal amount of money in the pot. Nobody should on any account make a joke about a *poultry sum*. Shoo the chicken away to a reasonable distance. What's a reasonable distance? About a stone's throw.

Next, pick up a stone.

Now, you all take turns hurling stones at that poor bird, which will squawk and flap and run about. The first person to hit the chicken wins all the money in the pot. You then agree never to mention any of this to an animal rights campaigner.

That's how the French played a game of chicken. The French, though, being French, called it a game of *poule*, which is French for chicken. And the chap who had won all the money had therefore won the *jeu de poule*.

The term got transferred to other things. At card games, the pot of money in the middle of the table came to be known as the *poule*. English gamblers picked the term up and brought it back with them in the seventeenth century. They changed the spelling to *pool*, but they still had a pool of money in the middle of the table.

It should be noted that this pool of money has absolutely nothing to do with a body of water. Swimming pools, rock pools and Liverpools are utterly different things.

Back to gambling. When billiards became a popular sport, people started to gamble on it, and this variation was known as *pool*, hence shooting pool. Then, finally, that poor French chicken broke free from the world of gambling and soared majestically out into the clear air beyond.

On the basis that gamblers *pooled* their money, people started to pool their resources and even pool their cars in a *car pool*. Then they pooled their typists in a *typing pool*. Le chicken was free! And then he grew bigger than any of us, because, since the phrase was invented in 1941, we have all become part of the *gene pool*, which, etymologically, means that we are all little bits of chicken.

Hydrogentlemanly

The gene of *gene pool* comes all the way from the ancient Greek word *genos*, which means birth. It's the root that you find in *generation, regeneration* and *degeneration*; and along with its Latin cousin *genus* it's scattered generously throughout the English language, often in places where you wouldn't expect it.

Take *generous*: the word originally meant *well-born*, and because it was obvious that well-bred people were magnanimous and peasants were stingy, it came to mean munificent. Indeed, the well-bred *gen*tleman established such a reputation for himself that the word *gentle*, meaning *soft*, was named after him. In fact, some gentlemen became so refined that the *gin* in *gingerly* is probably just another *gen* lurking in our language. *Gingerly* certainly has nothing to do with ginger.

Genos is hidden away in the very air that you breathe. The chemists of the late eighteenth century had an awful lot of trouble with the gases that make up the air. Oxygen, carbon dioxide, nitrogen and the rest all look exactly alike; they are transparent, they are effectively weightless. The only real difference anybody could find between them was their effects: what we now call oxygen makes things burn, while nitrogen puts them out.

Scientists spent a lot of time separating the different kinds of air and then had to decide what to call them all. Oxygen was called *flammable air* for a while, but it didn't catch on. It just didn't have the right scientific ring to it. We all know that scientific words need an obscure classical origin to make them sound impressive to those who wouldn't know an idiopathic craniofacial erythema* if it hit them in the face.

Eventually, a Frenchman named Lavoisier decided that the sort of air that produced water when it was burnt should be called the *water-producer*. Being a scientist, he of course dressed this up in Greek, and the Greek for water producer is *hydro-gen*. The bit of air that made things acidic he decided to call the *acid-maker* or *oxy-gen*, and the one that produced nitre then got called *nitro-gen*.

(Argon, the other major gas in air, wasn't known about at the time, because it's an inert gas and doesn't produce anything at all. That's why it's called argon. *Argon* is Greek for *lazy*.)

Most of the productive and reproductive things in the world have *gen* hidden somewhere in their names. All words are not homo*gen*ous and sometimes they are en*gen*dered in odd ways. For example, a group of things that reproduce is a *gen*us and if you're talking about a whole *gen*us then you're speaking in *gen*eral and if you're in *gen*eral command of the troops you're a *gen*eral and a *general* can order his troops to commit *gen*ocide, which, etymologically, would be suicide.

Of course, a general won't commit genocide himself; he'll

---

*That's a blush to you and me.

probably assign the job to his privates, and *privates* is a euphemism for *gonads*, which comes from exactly the same root, for reasons that should be too obvious to need explaining.

The Old and New Testicle

Gonads are *testicles* and testicles shouldn't really have anything to do with the Old and New *Testaments*, but they do.

The Testaments of the Bible *testify* to God's truth. This is because the Latin for *witness* was *testis*. From that one root, *testis*, English has inherited pro*test* (bear witness for), de*test* (bear witness against), con*test* (bear witness competitively), and *test*-icle. What are testicles doing there? They are *testi*fying to a man's virility. Do you want to prove that you're a real man? Well, your *testi*cles will *testi*fy in your favour.

That's the usual explanation, anyway. There's another, more interesting theory that in bygone days witnesses used to swear to things with their hands on their balls, or even on other people's balls. In the Book of Genesis, Abraham makes his servant swear not to marry a Canaanite girl. The King James Version has this translation:

I pray thee, thy hand under my thigh: And I will make thee swear by the LORD, the God of heaven, and the God of the earth

Now, that *may* be the correct translation, but the Hebrew doesn't say thigh, it says *yarek*, which means, approximately, *soft bits*. Nobody knows how oaths were sworn in the ancient world, but many scholars believe that people didn't put their hands on their hearts or their thighs, but on the testicles of the man to whom they were swearing, which would make the connection between *testis* and *testes* rather more direct.

Testicles. Bollocks. Balls. Nuts. Cullions. Cojones. Goolies. Tallywags. Twiddle-diddles. Bawbles, trinkets, spermaria. There are a hundred words for the danglers and they get everywhere. It's enough to make a respectable fellow blush. Do you enjoy the taste of avocado? So did I, until the terrible day when I realised that I was eating Aztec balls. You see, the Aztecs noticed the avocado's shape and decided that it resembled nothing so much as a big, green bollock. So they called it an *ahuakatl*, their word for testicle. When the Spanish arrived they misheard this slightly and called it *aguacate*, and the English changed this slightly to *avocado*. To remember that I used to like avocados with a touch of walnut oil only adds to my shame.

Even if you flee to an ivory tower and sit there wearing an orchid and a scowl, it still means that you have a testicle in your buttonhole, because that's what an orchid's root resembles, and *orchis* was the Greek for testicle. Indeed, the green-winged orchid used to rejoice in the name *Fool's Ballocks*. The technical term for somebody who has *a lot of balls* is a *polyorchid*.

And it's very possible that this *orb* on which we all live

comes from the same root as *orchid*, in which case we are whirling around the Sun on a giant testis, six billion trillion tons of gonad or *cod*, which is where *cod-philosophy*, *codswallop* and *codpiece* come from.

There are two codpieces at the top right of your computer keyboard, and how they got there is a rather odd story.

Parenthetical Codpieces

Your computer keyboard contains two pictures of codpieces, and it's all the fault of the ancient Gauls, the original inhabitants of France. Gauls spoke Gaulish until Julius Caesar came and cut them all into three parts. One of the Gaulish words that the Gauls used to speak was *braca* meaning trousers. The Romans didn't have a word for trousers because they all wore togas, and that's why the Gaulish term survived.

From *braca* came the early French *brague* meaning trousers, and when they wanted a word for a codpiece they decided to call it a *braguette* or *little trousers*. This is not to be confused with *baguette*, meaning stick. In fact, a Frenchman might brag that his baguette was too big for his braguette, but then Frenchmen will claim anything. They're *braggarts* (literally *one who shows off his codpiece*).

Braguettes were much more important in the olden days, especially in armour. On the medieval battlefield, with arrows flying hither and thither, a knight knew where he wanted the most protection. Henry VIII's codpiece, for example, was a gargantuan combination of efficiency and obscenity. It was big enough and shiny enough to frighten any enemy into disorganised retreat. It bulged out from the royal groin and stretched up to a metal plate that protected the royal belly.

And that is significant. What do you call the bit of stone that bulges out from a pillar to support a balcony or a roof? Until the sixteenth century nobody had been certain what to call them; but one day somebody must have been gazing at a cathedral wall and, in a moment of sudden clarity, realised that the architectural supports looked like nothing so much as Henry VIII's groin.

And so such architectural structures came to be known as *braggets*, and that brings us to Pocahontas.

Pocahontas was a princess of the Powhatan tribe, which lived in Virginia. Of course, the Powhatan tribe didn't *know* they lived in Virginia. They thought they lived in Tenakomakah, and so the English thoughtfully came with guns to explain their mistake. But the Powhatan tribe were obstinate and went so far as to take one of the Englishmen prisoner. They were planning to kill him until Pocahontas intervened with her father and Captain John Smith was freed. The story goes that she had fallen madly in love with him and that they had a passionate affair, but as Pocahontas was only ten years old at the time, we should probably move swiftly on.

Of course, it may not have happened exactly that way. The story has been improved beyond repair. But there definitely *was* a Pocahontas and there definitely *was* a Captain

John Smith, and they seem to have been rather fond of each other. Then he had an accident with one of his guns and had to return to England. The cruel colonists told Pocahontas that John Smith was dead, and she pined away in tears thinking that he was lost forever. In fact, he wasn't dead, he was writing a dictionary.

The Sea-Man's Grammar and Dictionary: Explaining all the Difficult Terms of Navigation hit the bookstands in 1627. It had all sorts of nautical jargon for the aspiring sailor to learn. But, for our story, the important thing is that Captain Smith spelt *braggets* as *brackets*, and the spelling stuck.

The original architectural device was called a bragget/bracket, because it looked like a codpiece. But what about a double bracket, which connects two horizontals to a vertical? An architectural double bracket looks like this: [

Look around you: there's probably one on the nearest bookshelf. And just as a physical bracket got its name because it resembled a codpiece, so the punctuation bracket got its name because it resembled the structural component.

In 1711 a man called William Whiston published a book called *Primitive Christianity Revived*. The book often quotes from Greek sources and when it does, it gives both Whiston's translation *and* the original in what he was the first man to call [brackets].

And that's why, if you look at the top right-hand corner of your computer keyboard, you will see two little codpieces [] lingering obscenely beside the letter P for *pants*.

Suffering for my Underwear

Once upon a time there was a chap who probably didn't exist and who probably wasn't called Pantaleon. Legend has it that he was personal physician to Emperor Maximianus. When the emperor discovered that his doctor was a Christian he got terribly upset and decreed that the doctor should die.

The execution went badly. They tried to burn him alive, but the fire went out. They threw him into molten lead but it turned out to be cold. They lashed a stone to him and chucked him into the sea, but the stone floated. They threw him to wild beasts, which were tamed. They tried to hang him and the rope broke. They tried to chop his head off but the sword bent and he forgave the executioner.

This last kindness was what earned the doctor the name *Pantaleon*, which means *All-Compassionate*.

In the end they got Pantaleon's head off and he died, thus becoming one of the *megalomartyrs* (the great martyrs) of Greece. By the tenth century Saint Pantaleon had become the patron saint of Venice. *Pantalon* therefore became a popular Venetian name and the Venetians themselves were often called the *Pantaloni*.

Then, in the sixteenth century, came the *Commedia Dell'Arte*: short comic plays performed by travelling troupes and always involving the same stock characters like Harlequin and Scaramouch.

In these plays Pantalone was the stereotypical Venetian. He was a merchant and a miser and a lustful old man, and he wore one-piece breeches, like Venetians did. These long breeches therefore became known as *pantaloons*. Pantaloons were shortened to *pants* and the English (though not the Americans) called their underwear *underpants*. *Underpants* were again shortened to *pants*, which is what I am now wearing.

Pants are all-compassionate. Pants are saints. This means that my underwear is named after an early Christian martyr.

Pans

So *pants* and *panties* come from Saint Pantaleon and your undies are all-compassionate and your small-clothes are martyred.

Saint Pantaleon was therefore a linguistic relation of Saint Pancras (who *held everything*) and Pandora, who was *given everything* in a box that she really shouldn't have opened.

Pan is one of those elements that gets everywhere. It's panpresent. For example, when a film camera *pans* across from one face to another, that *pan* comes from the same Greek word that you'll find in your underpants. Cinematic *panning* is short for the *panoramic camera*, which was patented back in 1868 and so called because a *panorama* is where you see everything.

A *panacea* cures absolutely everything, which is useful if you're in the middle of a *pandemic*, which is one up from an *epidemic*. An epidemic is only *among the people*, whereas a pandemic means *all the peoples of the world* are infected.

Pan also gives you all sorts of terribly useful words that for some reason loiter in dark and musty corners of the dictionary. *Pantophobia*, for example, is the granddaddy of all phobias as it means *a morbid fear of absolutely everything*. Pantophobia is the inevitable outcome of *pandiabolism*—the belief that the Devil runs the world—and, in its milder forms, is a *panpathy*, or *one of those feelings that everybody has now and then*.

However, not all *pans* mean *all*. It's one of the great problems of etymology that there are no hard and fast rules: nothing is panapplicable. The pans and pots in your kitchen have nothing whatsoever to do with panoramas and pan-Africanism. Panic is not a fear of everything; it is, in fact, the terror that the Greek god Pan, who rules the forests, is able to induce in anybody who takes a walk in the woods after dark. And the Greek god Pan is not panipotent. Nobody knows where his name comes from—all we're sure of is that he played the panpipes.

Back in 27 b.c., the Roman general Marcus Agrippa built a big temple on the edge of Rome and, in a fit of indecision, decided to dedicate it to all the gods at once. Six hundred years later the building was still standing and the Pope decided to turn it into a Christian church dedicated to Saint Mary and the Martyrs. Fourteen hundred years after that it's still standing and still has its original roof. Technically it's now called the Church of Saint Mary, but the tourists still call it the *Pantheon*, or *All the Gods*.

The exact opposite of the Pantheon is *Pandemonium*, the place of all the demons. These days pandemonium is just a word we use to mean that everything is a bit chaotic, but originally it was a particular palace in Hell. It was one of the hundreds of English words that were invented by John Milton.

Miltonic Meanders

A boring commentary in ten books of meandering verse
on the first chapter of Genesis . . .

. . . is how Voltaire described *Paradise Lost*, the great epic poem by John Milton. Voltaire was wrong, of course. *Paradise Lost* is mainly about Adam and Eve, and that pomavorous couple don't actually appear until the *second* chapter of the book of Genesis.

Paradise Lost is about the fall of Satan from Heaven and the fall of humanity from the Garden of Eden into the Land of Nod, and is generally speaking a downhill poem. However, it's still the greatest epic in English, an achievement that's largely due to its being almost the only epic in English that anybody has ever bothered writing, and certainly the only one that anyone has ever bothered reading. It's also the origin of *Pandemonium*.

In Milton's poem, when Satan is thrown out of Heaven and into Hell, the first thing he decides to do is to get a roof over his head. So he summons all the other fallen angels and gets them to build a huge and hideous palace. And just as the Pantheon is the temple of All the Gods, so Satan decides to name his new pied-à-terre *All the Demons* or *Pandemonium*, and that's how the word was invented.

Of course, since then pandemonium has come to mean anywhere that's a bit noisy, but it all goes back to Milton's idea, and his fondness for inventing language.

Milton adored inventing words. When he couldn't find the right term he just made one up: *impassive, obtrusive, jubilant, loquacious, unconvincing, Satanic, persona, fragrance, beleaguered, sensuous, undesirable, disregard, damp, criticise, irresponsible, lovelorn, exhilarating, sectarian, unaccountable, incidental* and *cooking*. All Milton's. When it came to inventive wording, Milton actually invented the word *wording*.

Awestruck? He invented that one too, along with *stunning* and *terrific*.

And, because he was a Puritan, he invented words for all the fun things of which he disapproved. Without dear old Milton we would have no *debauchery*, no *depravity*, no *extravagance*; in fact, nothing *enjoyable* at all.

Poor preachers! People always take their condemnations as suggestions. One man's abomination is another's good idea. This is the law of unintended consequences, and yes, Milton invented the word *unintended*. He probably didn't intend or imagine that one of his obscurer words would end up as the title for this book. *Etymologicon*, meaning a book containing etymologies, first crops up in his essay on *Nullities in Marriage*.

Whether you're *all ears* or obliviously *tripping the light fantastic*, you're still quoting Milton. "[T]rip it as ye go, / On the light fantastic toe" is from his poem *L'Allegro*. "In a light fantastic round" and "all ear" are from his play *Comus*. When a tennis player has an advantage, that's Milton's too, or at least he invented *advantage* in its sporting sense. When *all Hell breaks loose*, that's *Paradise Lost*, because when Satan escapes from Hell a curious angel asks him:

Wherefore with thee
Came not all Hell broke loose?

We rely on Milton. For example, he invented space travel, or at least made it linguistically possible. The word *space* had been around for centuries, but it was Milton who first applied it to the vast voids between the stars. Satan comforts his fallen angels by telling them that though they have been banned from Heaven,

Space may produce new worlds

And that's why we don't have *outer distance* or *void stations* or *expanse ships*. Because of Milton we have *2001: A Space Odyssey* and David Bowie's song "Space Oddity." Indeed, if there were any justice in pop music John Milton would be raking in the royalties from Jeff Beck's "Hi Ho Silver Lining," because Milton invented *silver linings*:*

> Was I deceived or did a sable cloud
> Turn forth her silver lining on the night?

This chapter is becoming rather *quotationist*, which is one of Milton's words that didn't catch on. So let us proceed to pastures new ("At last he rose and twitched his mantle blue,/Tomorrow to fresh woods and pastures new"). Let us forget about the silver linings and concentrate on the clouds.

Bloody Typical Semantic Shifts

Do you know the difference between the clouds and the sky? If you do, you're lucky, because if you live in England, the two are pretty much synonymous. The clouds aren't lined with silver. The weather is just miserable. It always has been and it always will be.

Our word *sky* comes from the Viking word for *cloud*, but in England there's simply no difference between the two

---

*He'd also be making a little less from Nick Cave's "Red Right Hand."

concepts, and so the word changed its meaning because of the awful weather.

If there's one thing that etymology proves conclusively, it's that the world is a wretched place. We may dream of better things, but the word *dream* comes from the Anglo-Saxon for *happiness*. There's a moral in that.

It has always rained, happiness has always been a dream, and people have always been lazy. I should know, I'm lazy myself. Ask me to do something like the washing up or a tax return and I'll reply that I'll do it *in five minutes*.

Five minutes usually means *never*.

If the task that I have been assigned is absolutely essential for my survival then I might say that I'll do it *in a minute*. That usually means *within an hour*, but I'm not guaranteeing anything.

Do not condemn me. Remember that a *moment* is the smallest conceivable amount of time. Now, turn on the radio or the television and wait. Soon enough an announcer will come on and say that "In a moment we'll be showing" this, that or the other, "but first the news and weather."

There's an old pop song by The Smiths called "How Soon is Now?" The writers of the song must have been even lazier than I am, because the answer is available in any etymological dictionary. *Soon* was the Anglo-Saxon word for *now*.

It's just that after a thousand years of people saying "I'll do that soon," *soon* has ended up meaning what it does today.

These days, *now* has to have a *right* stuck on the front or it doesn't mean a thing. The same happened to the word *anon* (not the shortening for *anonymous*, but the synonym for *soon*). It derives from the Old English phrase *on an*, which meant *on one* or *instantly*. But humans don't do things instantly, we just promise to. And the word *instantly* will, of course, go the way of its siblings.

And people are nasty, condemnatory creatures. The way people overstate the faults of others is, frankly, demonic. There's a lovely bit in *King Lear* where the Duke of Gloucester is having his eyes gouged out by Regan and responds by calling her a "naughty lady."

Naughty used to be a much more serious word than it is now, but it has been overused and lost its power. So many stern parents have called their children naughty that the power has slowly drained from the word. If you were naughty it used to mean that you were a *no-human*. It comes from exactly the same root as *nought* or *nothing*. Now it just means that you're mischievous.

Every weakness of human nature comes out in the history of etymology. Probably the most damning word is *probably*. Two thousand years ago the Romans had the word *probabilis*. If something was *probabilis* then it could be *proved by experiment*, because the two words come from the same root: *probare*.

But *probabilis* got overused. People are always more certain of things than they really should be, and that applied to the Romans just as much as to us. Roman lawyers would claim that their case was *probabilis*, when it wasn't. Roman astrologers would say that their predictions were *probabilis* when they weren't. And absolutely any sane Roman would tell you that it was *probabilis* that the Sun went round the Earth. So by the time poor *probably* first turned up in English in 1387 it was already a poor, exhausted word whose best days were behind it, and only meant *likely*.

Now, if *probable* comes from the same root as *prove*, can you guess why the proof of the pudding is in the eating?

The Proof of the Pudding

As we've seen, both *probable* and *prove* come from a single Latin root: *probare*. But while *probable* has, through overuse, come to mean only *likely*, *prove* has prospered and its meaning has grown stronger than it ever used to be. However, you can still see its humble origins in a few phrases that don't seem to make sense any more.

Why would an exception *prove the rule*? And why do you have a *proofreader*? What happens on a *proving ground* that is so very definitive? And what kind of rigorous philosopher would require *proof of a pudding*?

The answer to all of these can be found in that old Latin root: *probare*. Despite what was said in the last section, *probare* didn't exactly mean *prove* in our modern English sense, but it meant something very close. What the Romans did to their theories was to *test* them. Sometimes a theory would be tried and tested and found to work; other times a theory would be tried and tested and found wanting.

That's the same thing that happens to a book when it's sent to the proofreader. What the proofreader gets is a proof copy, which he pores over trying to fnid misspellings and unnecessary apostrophe's.

That's also why an exception really does prove a rule. The exception is what puts a rule to the test. That test may destroy it, or the rule may be tested and survive, but either way the theory has been *proved*.

Similarly, when a new weapon is taken to the proving ground, it's not just to make sure that it exists. The proving ground is a place where a weapon can be tested to make sure that it's as deadly as had been hoped.

All of which should explain why the *test* of a good dessert and the *proof of a pudding* is in the eating. It's the old sense of *prove*.

Mind you, you probably wouldn't have wanted to *prove* old puddings. A pudding was, originally, the entrails of an animal stuffed with its own meat and grease, boiled and stuck in a cupboard for later. One of the earliest recorded uses of the word is in a medieval recipe from 1450 for Porpoise Pudding:

Puddyng of Porpoise. Take the Blode of hym, & the grece of hym self, & Oatmeal, & Salt, & Pepir, & Gyngere, & melle [mix] these togetherys wel, & then put this in the Gut of the Porpoise, & then lat it seethe [boil] esyli, & not hard, a good while; & then take hym up, & broyle hym a lytil, & then serve forth.

The proof of porpoise pudding would definitely be in the eating. A pudding was effectively just a very strange (and possibly poisonous) kind of sausage.

Now, before the next link in the chain, can you take a guess as to why glamorous people put sausage poison in their faces?

Sausage Poison in Your Face

The Latin word for sausage was *botulus*, from which English gets two words. One of them is the lovely *botuliform*, which means *sausage-shaped* and is a more useful word than you might think. The other word is *botulism*.

Sausages may taste lovely, but it's usually best not to ask what's actually in them. Curiosity may have killed the cat, but it was a sausage-maker who disposed of the body. In nineteenth-century America, the belief that sausages were usually made out of dog meat was so widespread that they started to be called *hot dogs*, a word that survives to this day. Sausages are stuffed with pork and peril. They don't usually kill you, but they can.

There was an early nineteenth-century German called Justinus Kerner, who, when not writing rather dreary Swabian poetry, worked as a doctor. His poetry is now quite justifiably forgotten, but his medical work lives on. Kerner identified a new disease that killed some of his patients. It was a horrible malady that slowly paralysed every part of the body until the victim's heart stopped and he died. Kerner realised that all his dead patients had been eating cheap meat in sausages, so he decided to call the ailment *botulism*, or *sausage disease*. He also correctly deduced that bad sausages must contain a poison of some sort, which he called *botulinum toxin*.

In 1895 there was a funeral in Belgium. Ham was served to the guests at the wake and three of them dropped down dead. This must have delighted the undertakers, but it also meant that the remaining meat could be rushed to the University of Ghent. The professor of bacteria studied the homicidal ham under a microscope and finally identified the culprit, little bacteria that were, appropriately, shaped like sausages and are now called *Clostridium botulinum*.

This was an advance because it meant that Kerner's botulinum toxin could be manufactured. Now, you might be wondering why anybody would want to manufacture botulinum toxin. It is, after all, a poison. In fact, one microgram of it will cause near-instantaneous death by paralysis. But paralysis can sometimes be a good thing. If, for example, you're afflicted by facial spasms, then a doctor can inject a tinsy-winsy little dose of botulinum toxin into the affected area. A little, temporary paralysis kicks in, and the spasms are cured. Wonderful.

That, at least, was the original reason for manufacturing botulinum toxin; but very quickly people discovered that if you paralysed somebody's face it made them look a little bit younger. It also made them look very odd and incapable of expressing emotion, but who cares about that if you can remove a few years' worth of ageing?

Suddenly sausage poison was chic! The rich and famous couldn't get enough of sausage poison. It could extend a Hollywood actress's career by years. Old ladies could look middle-aged again! Injections of Kerner's sausage poison were like plastic surgery but less painful and less permanent. Sausage poison became the toast of Hollywood.

Of course, it's not called sausage poison anymore. That wouldn't be very glamorous. It's not even called botulinum toxin, because everybody knows that toxins are bad for you. Now that botulinum toxin has become chic, it's changed its name to *Botox*.

So, if Botox is sausage poison and *toxicology* is the study of poison and *intoxication* is poisoning, what does *toxophilite* mean?

Bows and Arrows and Cats

A *toxophilite* is somebody who loves archery. The reason for this is that *toxin* comes from *toxon*, the Greek word for *bow*, and *toxic* comes from *toxikos*, the Greek word for *pertaining to archery*. This is because in ancient warfare it was common practice to dip your arrowheads in poison. The two ideas were so connected in the Greek mind that *toxon* became *toxin*.

Archery used to be ubiquitous. That's why there are so many people called Archer, Fletcher (arrow-maker) and Bowyer (bow-maker) in the phone book. In 1363 Edward III passed a law that required all men over the age of fourteen and under the age of sixty to practise the sport once a week. Obviously, it wasn't so much a sport back then as a means of killing people. Edward III's law has never actually been repealed.

So, terms from archery are hidden all over the English language; for example, *upshot*. The *upshot* is the shot that decides who has won an archery contest. King Henry VIII's accounts for 1531 include his sporting losses and:

> To the three Cotons, for three sets which the King lost to them in Greenwich Park £20, and for one upshot won of the King.

Tudor archery was not necessarily a pleasant business. There are two theories on the origin of the phrase *enough room to swing a cat*. The first is that the *cat* is a cat-o'-nine-tails and that it's hard to whip somebody properly in a small room. The other theory is to do with marksmanship.

Hitting a stationary target was just too easy for the Tudors. So the best archers used to test themselves by putting a cat in a bag and hanging the bag from the branch of a tree. The ferocious feline would wriggle about and the sack would swing, and this exercise in animal cruelty provided the discerning archer with a challenge and English with a phrase.

Incidentally, this has nothing to do with *letting the cat out of the bag*. That's to do with pigs, obviously. In medieval markets piglets were sold in sacks, so that the farmer could carry them home more easily. This was *a pig in a poke*. A standard con at the time involved switching a valuable piglet for a valueless cat or dog. You were then being *sold a pup*, or, if you discovered the trick, you would *let the cat out of the bag*. Unlikely as that all sounds, there are equivalent phrases in almost every European language.

But to return to archery, all this sagittopotent* and toxophilite tosh brings us around to the odd phrase *point blank*.

The *blank* here is not your usual English *blank*, though it's closely related. The *blank* in *point blank* is the French *blanc*, which of course means *white*. The term *bullseye* is reasonably new. It was invented only in the nineteenth century. Before that, the white spot bang in the middle of an archery target was called the *white* or *blank*.

The funny thing about archery is that you don't usually aim at the target. Gravity decrees that if you aim straight at the blank your arrow will hit somewhere below. So you point the arrow somewhere above the blank, and hope that this cancels out the effects of Newton's troublesome invention.

---

*Good at archery, like Sagittarius, but we'll come to the Zodiac (or *little zoo*) later.

That's why *aim high* is another archer's term; it doesn't mean that you'll end up high, or it's not meant to. You aim high and hit on the level.

However, there's one situation in which this rule does not apply: if you are very, very, very, very close to the target. In that case you can aim straight at the *blank point* or white spot in the middle. If you're that close to the target, you're at *point blank* range.

Black and White

Etymologists have a terrible time distinguishing black from white. You'd think that the two concepts could be kept apart, but that wasn't how the medieval English thought about things. They were a confusing bunch of people and must have had a terrible time ordering coffee. The *Oxford English Dictionary* itself feebly admits that: "In Middle English it is often doubtful whether *blac, blak, blacke*, means 'black, dark,' or 'pale, colourless, wan, livid.' "

Chess would have been a confusing game; but on the plus side, racism must have been impractical.

Utterly illogical though all this may sound, there are two good explanations. Unfortunately, nobody is quite sure which one is true. So I shall give you both.

Once upon a time, there was an old Germanic word for

burnt, which was *black*, or as close to *black* as makes no difference. The confusion arose because the old Germanics
couldn't decide between black and white as to which colour
burning was. Some old Germans said that when things were
burning they were bright and shiny, and other old Germans
said that when things were *burnt* they turned black.

The result was a hopeless monochrome confusion, until
everybody got bored and rode off to sack Rome. The English
were left holding *black*, which could mean either *pale* or *dark*,
but slowly settled on one usage. The French also imported this
useless *black* word. They then put an N in it and later sold it on
to the English as *blank*, leaving us with *black* and *blank* as
opposites.

The other theory (which is rather less likely, but still good
fun) is that there was an old German word *black* which meant
bare, *void* and *empty*. What do you have if you don't have any
colours?

Well, it's hard to say really. If you close your eyes you see
nothing, which is *black*, but a *blank* piece of paper is, usually,
white. Under this theory, *blankness* is the original sense and
the two colours—*black* and *white*—are simply different
interpretations of what *blank* means.

And, just to prove the point even more irritatingly, *bleach*
comes from the same root and can mean *to make pale*, or any
substance used for making things black. Moreover, *bleak* is
probably just a variant of *bleach* and once meant white.

Such linguistic nonsenses are a lot more common than
you might reasonably have hoped. *Down* means *up*. Well,

okay, it means *hill*, but hills are upward sorts of things, aren't they? In England there's a range of hills called the Sussex Downs. This means that you can climb up a down.

Down, as in *fall down*, was originally *off-down*, meaning *off-the-hill*. So if an Old Englishman fell off the top of a hill he would fall *off-down*. Then lazy Old Englishmen started to drop the word *off*. Rather than saying that they were going *off-down*, they just started going *down*. So we ended up with the perplexing result that the *downs* are *up* above you, and that going *downhill* is really going *downdown*.

But we must get back to *blanks* and lotteries.

Once upon a time, a lottery worked like this. You bought a ticket and wrote your name on it. Then you put it into the name jar. Once all the tickets had been sold, another jar was filled up with an equal number of tickets, on some of which were written the name of a prize.

The chap running the lottery would pull out two tickets, one from the name jar and one from the prize jar. Thus, way back in 1653, the court of King James I was described as:

A kind of Lotterie, where men that venture much may draw a Blank, and such as have little may get the Prize.

Blank lottery tickets were thus the financial opposite of *blank cheques* (if you're British) and *blank checks* (if you're American), although as we shall see, the American spelling is older.

Hat Cheque Point Charlie

Almost every word in the English language derives from *shah*.

Once upon a time, Persia was ruled by shahs. Some shahs were happy shahs. Other shahs were crippled or dead. In Persian that meant that they were *shah mat*. *Shah* went into Arabic as, well, *shah* (ain't etymology fascinating?). That went into Vulgar Latin as *scaccus*. That went into vulgar French (all French is vulgar) as *eschec* with the plural *esches*, and that went into English as *chess*, because a game of chess is a *game of king*, the king being the most important piece on the board. And what happened to *shah mat*? When the king is crippled, a chess player still says *checkmate*.

Chess is played on a chessboard. Chessboards are kind of useful because you can arrange stuff on them. For example, when Henry II wanted to do his accounts he did them on:

> a quadrangular surface about ten feet in length, five in breadth, placed before those who sit around it in the manner of a table, and all around it it has an edge about the height of one's four fingers, lest any thing placed upon it should fall off. There is placed over the top of the escheker, moreover, a cloth bought at the Easter term, not an ordinary one but a black one marked with stripes, the stripes being distant from each other the space of a foot or the breadth of a hand. In the spaces moreover are counters placed according to their values.
>
> *Dialogus de Scaccario*, c. 1180

It looked just like a chessboard and, as Henry II spoke French, it was called the *Escheker*—that's why the finances of the British government are still controlled by the *Chancellor of the Exchequer*. (The S changed to X through confusion and foolishness.)

But chess and Persian kings don't stop there. We are nowhere near the endgame. Let us continue unchecked.

You see, when your opponent puts you in *check*, your options become very limited. You have to get out of *check* in one move or it's *checkmate* and the game is over. From this you get the idea of somebody or something being *held in check*. *Checking* somebody *stops* them doing what they want, and that's why you can still body-*check* people, and why government is held *in check* by *checks and balances*.

Check or *cheque* began to mean somebody who stopped things going wrong. For example, the *Clerk of the Cheque*, whom Pepys mentions in his seventeenth-century diaries, was the chap who kept a separate set of accounts for the royal shipyard. He *checked* fraud and served a good lunch.

> I walked and enquired how all matters and businesses
> go, and by and by to the Clerk of the Cheque's house,
> and there eat some of his good Jamaica brawne.

And from that you get the sense of a *check* as something that stops dishonesty. At a *hat-check*, for example, you get a *check* to prove that you're not stealing somebody else's hat. Bank *checks* (or *cheques*) were originally introduced as a replacement for promissory notes and got their name because they *checked* fraud.

Bank checks started out being spelled with a *–ck* on both sides of the Atlantic. But British people, perhaps under the influence of the Chancellor of the Exchequer, decided to start calling them cheques. This has a peculiar etymological result. A *blank cheque* is a *cheque* with no *check* on it. Given that blank cheques are found from as early as 1812, it's a miracle that the first *bouncing cheque* isn't recorded in the dictionary until 1927.

And from there you get *check off* (1839) and *check up* (1889). And then the Wright Brothers invented the aeroplane and people would fly around and navigate by distinctive landmarks called *checkpoints*. And then the Second World War broke out and pilots were trained and given an examination or *checkout*. Then shops got *checkouts* and *roadblocks* became *checkpoints* and people went to doctors for *checkups* and guests *checked out* of hotels and *checked in* at *check-ins* wearing a *checked* shirt and all, dear reader, *all* because of crippled shahs from ancient Persia.

All of this has nothing to do with the Czech Republic, which is ruled not by a shah but a president. However, Ivan Lendl's wife could reasonably be said to have a *Czech mate*.

Sex and Bread

Freud said that everything was secretly sexual. But etymologists know that sex is secretly food.

For example, *mating* with somebody was originally just sharing your food, or *meat*, with them (*meat* meant food of any kind and not just flesh). Likewise, your *companion* is somebody with whom you share your *bread* (from the Latin *panis*).

The Old English word for bread was *hlaf*, from which we get *loaf*; and the Old English division of labour was that women made bread and men guarded it. The woman was therefore the *hlaf-dige* and the man was the *hlaf-ward*.

Hlafward and Hlafdige
Hlaford and Hlafdi
Lavord and Lavedi
Lord and Lady

And Indian bread is in the nude, but to explain that I'm going to have to explain how half the languages in the world began, or at least the best theory on the subject.

Once upon a terribly long time ago, four thousand years before the birth of Jesus of Nazareth, there were some fellows living between the Black Sea and the Caspian. Whenever one of them died the others would bury him, or her, in a pit. They were therefore called the Kurgan Pit Burial culture. They also had some distinctive pottery and all the other tedious accoutrements of Neolithic man.

Well, *we* call them the Kurgans. We don't know what they called themselves. This was in the time before the invention of writing, or even of the internet, so we don't know what language they spoke, but we can take a very educated guess, and that educated guess is called *Proto-Indo-European*, or PIE for short.

The Kurgans probably invented the chariot, and probably used it to invade their neighbours. However, they did these invasions in a deplorably disorganised manner. Rather than all banding together and attacking in one direction, they split up and attacked hither and thither. Some of them ended up in northern India and some of them ended up in Persia. Some went to the cold, rainy lands around the Baltic, and some of them went to Greece and became Greek. Still others got lost and ended up in Italy and it was, to put it gently, a big mess.

We can tell where they went by digging up their burial pits and their distinctive pottery and whatnot. But their pottery is not what makes them interesting. They also took with them their language—Proto-Indo-European—and spread it all over Europe and Asia.

One would have hoped that this would operate like a reverse Tower of Babel, but it did not. You see, all the different groups developed different accents and these accents became so strong that their languages became mutually incomprehensible. After a few hundred years the Kurgans in northern India wouldn't have been able to make out what their cousins in Italy were saying. If you want to see this process in action today, visit Glasgow.

So the ancient Indians called their dads *pitar*, and the Greeks called their dads *pater*, and the Romans called them *pater*. The Germans, though, started pronouncing the letter P in a very funny way that made it sound more like an F. So they called their male parent *fater*, and we call him *father*, because English is descended from Old German.

Similarly, the PIE word *seks* became German *sechs*, English *six*, Latin *sextus*, Sanskrit *sas* and Greek *hex*; because the Greeks pronounced their Ss funny.

There are rules of pronunciation like the German P-F and the Greek S-H that mean we can trace all these fundamental words. That's how we can work back and take an educated guess about what Proto-Indo-European was. However, it isn't always so simple.

Just looking at changes in pronunciation works very well on the great unchanging concepts like fathers and numbers. However, many words change their meaning as they go along. Let's look at the Proto-Indo-European word *neogw*, which meant *unclothed*.

In the German languages (of which English is one) *neogw* became *naked*. In the Latin languages *neogw* became *nude*. But a funny thing happened in Persia to do with cookery.

You see, the ancient Persians cooked their meat by burying it in hot ashes. However, they baked their bread *uncovered* in an oven. They still used the PIE *neogw*, and therefore called their bread *nan*.

Nan was taken into Hindi as *naan*, and if you go into an Indian restaurant today you can still buy a lovely, puffy sort of bread called *naan*, and it's etymologically *naked*.

Some bread names are even stranger. *Ciabatta* is the Italian for *slipper*, *matzoh* means *sucked out*, and *pumpernickel* means *Devil-fart*.

Now what has *Pumpernickel* got to do with *partridge*?

Concealed Farts

Aubrey's *Brief Lives* contains this sad story about the seventeenth Earl of Oxford:

> This Earle of Oxford, making of his low obeisance to Queen Elizabeth, happened to let a Fart, at which he was so abashed and ashamed that he went to Travell, 7 yeares. On his return the Queen welcomed him home and sayd, My Lord, I had forgot the Fart.

Farts are quickly delivered and slowly forgotten. The English language, though, has had much more than seven years to let the world forget its flatulence. The smell of the original meaning slowly peters out.

Take, for example, the phrase *peter out*. Nobody is quite sure where it comes from, but one of the best theories is that it comes from the French *peter*, which meant *fart*. *Peter* definitely gave us the word *petard*, meaning *a little explosive*, for reasons that should be obvious to anyone who has eaten beans.

However, when Hamlet says, "'Tis sport to have the engineer hoist with his own petard," he doesn't mean that the poor engineer is raised into the air by the jet power of his own flatulence, but that he's blown upward by his own explosive. The fart had ceased to smell.

The same thing has happened with the phrase *fizzle out*, which once meant cutting the cheese and was delicately described in one nineteenth-century dictionary as "an escape backwards." The same dictionary describes a *fice* as:

> A small windy escape backwards, more obvious to the nose than ears; frequently by old ladies charged [blamed] on their lap-dogs.

And *fice* itself comes from the Old English *fist*, which likewise meant fart. In Elizabethan times a smelly dog was called a *fisting cur*, and by the eighteenth century any little dog was called a *feist*, and that's where we get the word *feisty* from. Little dogs are so prone to bark at anything that an uppity girl was called *feisty*, straight from the flatulent dogs of yore. This is a point well worth remembering when you're next reading a film review about a "feisty heroine."

The fart lingers.

Our word *partridge* comes from the Old French *pertis* which comes from the Latin *perdix* which comes from the Greek *perdix* which comes from the Greek verb *perdesthai* which means *fart*, because that's what a partridge sounds like when it flies. The low, loud beating of the wings sounds like the clapping of the buttocks when the inner gale is liberated.

A polite, even beautiful, word for foods that make your bottom quack is *carminative*. There used to be carminative medicines, for it was widely believed that farting was good for you, as in the rhyme:

Beans, beans, they're good for the heart
The more you eat, the more you fart;
The more you fart, the better you feel;
So let's have beans for every meal.

This belief in the curative powers of flatulence was, originally, based on the idea of humours. The body was thought to be filled with substances that could get horribly out of balance. A fart was like a comb or card being pulled through wool and removing the knots. The Latin for a wool card was *carmen*, which has nothing to do with the opera, but is exactly the same as *heckling*.

Wool

Heckling is, or once was, the process of removing the knots from wool. Sheep are notoriously lackadaisical about their appearance, so before their wool can be turned into a nice warm sweater it must be combed.

It's easy to see how combing wool and teasing out the knots could be used metaphorically for *combing* through an oration and *teasing* the orator, but the connection is probably far more direct and goes to the Scottish town of Dundee.

Dundee was a radical place in the eighteenth century. It was the local centre of the wool trade and was therefore overrun with hecklers. The hecklers were the most radical workers of all. They formed themselves into what today would be called a trade union and used collective bargaining to guarantee themselves good pay and perks. The perks were mostly in the form of alcohol, but that was to be expected.

They were a political lot, the hecklers. Every morning while most of them were busy heckling, one of their number would stand up and read aloud from the day's news. They thus formed strong opinions on all subjects and when politicians and dignitaries tried to address them, their speeches were combed over with the same thoroughness as the wool. Thus *heckling*.

Wool is everywhere in language. If you possess a mobile phone you are probably wooling your friends every day without even realising it. You are, after all, currently reading wool.

Or had you never noticed the connection between *text* and *textile*?

That you send woolly messages on your telephone and read wool and cite wool from the Bible is all down to a Roman orator named Quintilian. Quintilian was the greatest orator of his day, so great that the Emperor Domitian appointed him as tutor to his two grand-nephews who were also his heirs. Nobody knows what exactly Quintilian taught them, but Domitian soon sent them both into exile.

The two lines of Quintilian that interest us are in the *Institutio Oratorico*, a gargantuan twelve-volume work on absolutely everything to do with rhetoric. In it, Quintilian says that after you have chosen your words you must weave them together into a fabric—*in textu iungantur*—until you have a fine and delicate *text*[*ure*[*ile*]] or *textum tenue atque rasum*.

It's the sort of thing we say all the time. We *weave* stories together and *embroider* them and try never to lose the *thread* of the story. Quintilian's metaphor lasted. Late classical writers took up *text* to mean any short passage in a book and then we took it to mean anything that was written down and then somebody invented the SMS message. This sheepskin writing is all rather appropriate, given that the size of books depends upon the size of sheep.

Paper was invented in China about two thousand years ago, but we in the West didn't take up the invention until the fourteenth century. Even then, paper was considered an oriental oddity. The first English paper mill was founded in 1588.

Before paper, readers had to make do with one of two alternatives. They could use the papyrus plant, which grew plentifully in Egypt. If you mashed up papyrus you could make something that resembled paper—indeed, it was similar enough that *papyr*us is where we get the word *paper*.

Unfortunately, there's very little papyrus in England. Instead, we used sheepskins, and now you can too. Here's the recipe.

1. Take one sheep.
2. Kill it and skin it (it's vital to do this in the right order).
3. Wash the bloody skin in water, then soak it in beer for a couple of days until the hair falls out.
4. Let it dry stretched out on a wooden rack called a *tenter*. To keep it taut and flat, attach it using *tenterhooks*.
5. After a couple of days you should have something that's approximately rectangular with four sad extrusions that used to be legs.
6. Cut off legs and discard.
7. Trim the remainder down until you have an exact rectangle.
8. Fold in half.
9. You should now have four pages (printed front and back) that are roughly the size of a modern atlas. This is called a folio. All you now need to make an atlas of more than four pages is more sheep.
10. Fold it in half again and you'll have eight pages at roughly the size of a modern encyclopedia. You'll need to slice the pages at the top to make the pages turnable. This is called a quarto.
11. Fold again.
12. Provided you started off with an average-sized medieval sheep, you should now be holding something pretty much the size of a hardback novel. This is called an octavo.
13. Fold again.
14. Mass-market paperback.

When Caxton built his printing press in the fifteenth century, he set it up to use sheepskin and not paper. When paper was finally introduced it was manufactured to fit the existing printing presses, and that's the reason that both the text you're reading and the book that contains it are dependent upon sheep.

Of course, you may be reading this on your e-book reader, but as those have been designed to mimic the size of normal books, you're still at the mercy of the sheep.

Wool gets everywhere in language. Muslim mystics are called *Sufis* because of the woollen, or *suf*, garments that they wore. *Burlesque* dancers on the other hand are taking part in a nonsensical or trifling show named after the Latin *burra* meaning *a tuft of wool*. Burras were used as coverings for desks, and that gave us *bureaus* and then *bureaucracies*.

Then there are all different kinds of wool: cashmere came originally from Kashmir and Angora came from Ankara, the capital of Turkey.

Turkey is, of course, the country you eat for Christmas.

Turkey

Early explorers in the Americas saw flocks of turkeys singing in the magnolia forests, for the turkey is native to America. Indeed, it was domesticated and eaten by the Aztecs. Why it should therefore be named after a country in Asia Minor is a little odd, but explicable.

Many animals are misnamed. Guinea pigs, for example, aren't pigs and they aren't from Guinea. They are found in *Guyana* in South America, and it takes only a little mispronunciation to move them across the Atlantic. The pig bit is just weird.

The same is true of the helmeted guinea fowl, or *Numidia meleagris*, which was once native to Madagascar but not Guinea. The helmeted guinea fowl is an ugly bird. It has a big bony knob on the top of its head (hence the name), but it tastes *delicious*.

People started importing helmeted guinea fowl from Madagascar to Europe, and the people who did the importing were usually Turkish traders. They were known as Turkey merchants, and the birds that they brought were therefore called *turkeys*. But those aren't the turkeys that we eat at Christmas with bread sauce and relatives. That bird is *Meleagris gallopavo*, which is also delicious.

It was the Spanish conquistadors who found *Meleagris gallopavo* in the magnolia forests and brought it back to Europe. It became popular in Spain and then in North Africa. And though it's a different species from the helmeted guinea fowl, the two birds do look surprisingly alike.

People got confused. The birds looked the same, tasted similar and both were exotic new dishes brought from Somewhere Foreign. So it was assumed that they were the same thing, and the American bird got called turkey as well, in the mistaken belief that it was a bird that was mistakenly believed to come from Turkey.

In Turkey itself, of course, they didn't make this mistake. They knew the bird wasn't theirs. So the Turks made a completely different mistake and called it a *hindi*, because they thought the bird was probably Indian. The French thought the same and they still call turkey *dindon* or *d'Inde*, which also means *from India*. It's a most confusing bird but delicious.

In fact, it was so delicious that, though it was introduced to England only in the 1520s or 30s, it had become the standard Christmas meal by the 1570s. None of which explains why people occasionally *talk turkey*. Indeed, they demand to talk turkey. This all goes back to an old joke, that isn't, I'm afraid, very funny.

The joke involves a turkey and a buzzard. Now, it may be possible to eat buzzard. I don't know. But the bird's absence from any menu that I've ever encountered makes me suspicious. I suspect the buzzard is a foul fowl, and that's certainly the point of the story.

Once upon a time, a white man and a Red Indian went out hunting together. They killed a tasty turkey and a buzzard. So the white man said to his companion: "You take the buzzard and I'll take the turkey, or, if you prefer, I can take the turkey and you can take the buzzard."

To which the Red Indian replied: "You don't talk turkey at all."

This joke was immensely popular in nineteenth-century America. It was even quoted in Congress, though history doesn't recall whether anybody laughed. But it was popular enough to spawn *two* phrases.

By 1919 *talking turkey* had been altered somewhat: people had started inserting the adjective *cold*. *Talking cold turkey* is like talking turkey only more so. You were getting beyond the brass tacks and down to the barest of bare essentials. Talking cold turkey was the bluntest, directest form of speech.

And a couple of years later, in 1921, people started to use the phrase *cold turkey* to describe the bluntest, most direct method of giving up drugs.

So *going cold turkey* has nothing whatsoever to do with the miserable leftovers so sorrowfully consumed in the week after Christmas. Cold turkey isn't a food at all, even though it sounds like one. It's a blunt way of talking, and a blunt way of giving up drugs.

However, when you *give someone the cold shoulder*, that is a food.

Insulting Foods

There are two sorts of guests: welcome and unwelcome. The host is not permitted to tell you which you are, though he may give you a clue.

If your host cooks you a nice hot dinner, you're probably welcome. If he gives you yesterday's leftovers—for example, a *cold shoulder* of mutton—then he probably wishes you hadn't come around.

It could have been worse, though—he could have made you eat *humble pie*. Humble pie is made using the *umbles* or innards of a deer. Here's a recipe from Nathan Bailey's *Dictionarium Domesticum* of 1736:

> Boil the umbles of a deer until they are very tender, set them by till they are cold, and chop them as small as meat for minc'd pyes, and shred to them as much beef suet, six large apples and half a pound of currants, as much sugar; seasoning with salt, pepper, cloves and nutmegs, according to your palate; mix all well together, and when you put them into the paste, pour in half a pint of sack, the juice of one orange and two lemons, then close the pie, bake it, and serve it hot to table.

Of course, the umbles are the worst parts of the deer. After a hard day's stag-hunting a rich man will dine on venison. Only his servants beneath the stairs would have to make do with umble (and therefore humble) pie.

Folk Etymology

The addition of the H to *umble* is an example of what's known as folk etymology. Somebody who didn't know what an *umble* was saw the words *umble pie* and got confused. Then they saw that umble pie was a humble dish, assumed that somebody had just missed off the H, and decided to put it back. Thus umble pie becomes humble pie. That's folk etymology.

A *duckling* is a little duck and a *gosling* is a little goose and a *darling* is a little dear, and on the same principle a little fellow who stood at an important chap's side used to be known as a *sideling*.

Then the origin of the word *sideling* was forgotten and in the seventeenth century people decided that it must be the participle of a verb, just as *leaping* and *sleeping* are participles of *leap* and *sleep*. There was only one problem with this theory: there didn't seem to be a verb to fit the noun. So one was invented and from then on a *sideling* became somebody who *sidled*. These days there aren't nearly as many lords and servant boys and so *sideling* itself has vanished. People still *sidle around* and *sidle up* to each other, but they are able to do so only because of a mistake of folk etymology and the backformation of a new word.

Another common form of folk etymology happens when people alter the spelling of strange or unfamiliar words so that they appear to make more sense. For example, there's a drowsy little rodent that the French therefore used to call a *dormeuse*, which meant *she who sleeps*. In English we call the same creature a *dormouse*. That's despite the fact that it isn't a mouse and has no particular affinity for doors. The reason is that the English had *field mice* and *town mice* and so they were, of course, going to look at the word *dormeuse* and conclude that someone just didn't know how to spell.

The same principle applies to fairies, or rather to the disappearance of fairies. Once upon a time, belief in fairies was commonplace. They lived not at the bottom of the garden, but in the woods, where they would play all sorts of mysterious games. They would milk people's cattle in the night, or hide in flowers and under trees, and generally do the sorts of things that would get you or me arrested. They were known as the Folks. When it was cold the Folks liked to wear gloves, which is why there is, or used to be, a flower called a *folks' glove*.

But the fairies have all died (or maybe just got better at hiding) and people stopped referring to them as Folks many years ago, which is why the name *folks' glove* became rather peculiar. Then some clever fellow decided that they weren't *folks' gloves* after all, they must be *fox-gloves* because foxes have such dinky little feet, and the error set in. They are foxgloves now, and foxgloves they will remain, until somebody makes a better mistake.

By the same system, the old word *crevis* is now spelled and pronounced *crayfish*, even though it's not very fishlike. The Spanish *cucaracha* became a *cockroach*, and most wonderfully of all, the Indian *mangus* became a *mongoose*, although there's not a huge similarity between the furry, snake-devouring mammal and a goose.

An exception to these folk etymologies is the *butterfly*. Butterflies do have something to do with butter, although nobody is quite sure what. They like to flutter around milk pails and butter churns, which might explain it. Many butterflies are yellow, which would be a good reason for the name. But there's another, more troubling possibility: butterflies, like the rest of us, are subject to the call of the lavatory, and butterfly poo is yellow, just like butter.

Now, you may ask yourself, what sort of person goes around peering at butterfly poo and then naming an insect after it? The answer, it would appear, is that Dutch people do that. Or at least, an old Dutch word for butterfly was *boterschijte*.

Of course, you may dismiss that last theory as poppycock, but if you do, please remember that *poppycock* comes from the Dutch *pappe-cack*, meaning *soft shit*.

Before the next link, can you guess what butterflies have to do with psychiatry and pasta?

Butterflies of the World

For some reason the languages of the world put more effort into the names of butterflies than those of any other creature. From Norway to Malaysia the words are extraordinary.

Malay doesn't have plurals like ours. In English you simply add an S to the end of the word. But in Malay you form your plural by repeating the noun, so *tables* would become *table table*. It's a system with some sort of logic to it. When there's more than one word, that means there's more than one thing.

It works out fine for the speaker of Malay, so long as the original singular noun wasn't formed by reduplication itself, as is the case with their butterflies. The Malay for *butterfly* is *rama-rama*, so *butterflies* is *rama-rama rama-rama*. And it doesn't stop there. The Malays also repeat verbs to intensify them, so *I really like* would be rendered as *I like like*, or *suka suka*. We occasionally do this in English, when somebody says, "I've got to, *got to* see that film." All of which means that the Malay for *I love butterflies* is:

Saya suka suka rama-rama rama-rama

In Italian, butterflies are called *farfalle* and there's a kind of butterfly-shaped pasta named after them that you can buy in most supermarkets. Outside Italy, though, most people don't realise that it's *butterfly pasta*, and in America they ignore the Italian name entirely and call *farfalle bow ties*, because a butterfly resembles a bow tie, and in an emergency could probably serve as a substitute.

This is a point of dress not lost upon the Russians, who call a bow tie a butterfly. And as a butterfly is, in Russian, a little lady, bow ties, butterflies and girls are all called *babochkas* (like *babushkas*).

In the bleak Norwegian winter there are no butterflies at all, so when they emerge from their chrysalises in the bleak Norwegian summer they are called *summer-birds, or somerfogl*.

In French they rather boringly just took the Latin *papilio* and called their butterflies *papillons*. But then, in a fit of inventiveness, they realised that the grand tents in which kings sat at tournaments and jousts were shaped like the wings of a butterfly, so they called them *papillons*, and we call them *pavilions*, which means that there's a butterfly at one end of Lord's Cricket Ground.

Why all these intricate and exquisite names? Nobody bothers with the humble fly (which does exactly what it says on the tin) or the beetle (*biter*) or the bee (*quiverer*), or the lousily named louse. Butterflies hog all the attention of the word-makers.

Perhaps this is because in many quite distinct and unconnected cultures the butterfly is imagined to be a human soul that has shaken off this mortal coil of woes and now flutters happily through a gaily coloured afterlife.

This was the belief of the Maoris, and of the Aztecs in whose mythology Itzpapalotl was the goddess of the Obsidian Butterfly: a soul encased in stone who could be freed only by another tongue-twisting god called Tezcatlipoca.

There also seems to have been a ghost of this belief among the ancient Greeks. The Greek for butterfly was *psyche*, and Psyche was the goddess of the soul. There's a lovely allegorical poem about her called "Cupid and Psyche," and she's also the origin of the *study of the soul*: *psychoanalysis*.

Psychoanalysis and the Release of the Butterfly

The great thing about creating something is that you get to give it a name. Who would endure the expense and incontinence of babies, were it not for the fun of saddling another human with a moniker that you chose yourself?

With this in mind one can imagine Sigmund Freud sitting in his study in Vienna and considering Psyche, the Greek goddess of the soul and mystical butterfly. That's what he was analysing (with the stress on the first two syllables), so he decided to call his new invention psychoanalysis. *Analysis* is Greek for *release*. So Freud's new art would be, literally, the *liberation of the butterfly*. How pretty! Freud was probably so pleased with himself that he became lazy, for most of the other psychological terms are Jungian.

Carl Jung was Freud's protégé. Then one day Carl had a dream that wasn't about sex. He hesitated before telling Freud something quite that embarrassing. Confessing to a psychoanalyst that you've had an innocent dream is rather like confessing to your grandmother that you've had a dirty one. Freud was outraged. What sort of fruitcake, he demanded, has a dream that isn't dirty? It was inconceivable. Freud decided that Jung had gone quite mad, that the dream really had been dirty, and that Jung was just being coy.

Jung insisted that his dream wasn't about sex and that, in fact, it was about his grandparents being hidden in a cellar. So he rejected Freud's pansexualism (not a sin of cookery, but the belief that everything comes down to nooky) and ran off to become a Jungian.

Having invented his own form of psychoanalysis, Jung now had naming rights. So it was Carl and not Sigmund who decided that a psychological problem should be called a *complex*. Then he thought up *introverts* and *extroverts*, and finally, realising that naming was a doddle, he invented *synchronicity* and *ambivalent*. And with that he sat down to rest on his laurels and consider his subterranean grandparents.

But the grand panjandrum and greatest inventor of psychological terms was neither Sigmund Freud nor Carl Jung. It was a man who was just as important but is far less known today: Richard von Krafft-Ebing.

Krafft-Ebing was born sixteen years before Dr. Freud and 35 years before Jung. He was, essentially, the first doctor to start writing case histories of people whose sexual behaviour wasn't entirely respectable.

The book that resulted, *Psychopathia Sexualis* (1886), was so scandalous that large chunks of it had to be written in Latin, in order to keep it out of the hands of the prurient public. The idea was that if you were clever enough to understand Latin, you couldn't possibly be a pervert (something that nobody mentioned to Caligula).

Because Krafft-Ebing was a pioneer he had to invent terms left, right and centre. Humanity had a long history of condemning peccadilloes, but not of classifying them. So it was in the translation of *Psychopathia Sexualis* that English first got the words *homosexual, heterosexual, necrophilia, frotteur, anilingus, exhibitionism, sadism* and *masochism*.

Sadism had, in fact, been around for a while in French. The French writer Donatien Alphonse François Marquis de Sade was famous for producing horrid books about people being horrid to each other in bed. Really horrid. Catchy titles like *One Hundred and Twenty Days of Sodom* should give you some idea, but a clearer image of the nature of Sade's work comes from the fact that in the 1930s a historian by the name of Geoffrey Gorer, who was researching the marquis, went to the British Museum to read some of de Sade's works that were stored there. However, he was told by the British Museum that it was a rule that people were only allowed to read de Sade's books "in the presence of the Archbishop of Canterbury and two other trustees."

So it's easy to see how de Sade's notoriety meant that his favourite activity became known as *sadism* in French. But Richard von Krafft-Ebing also needed a name for sadism's opposite: masochism.

Leopold von Sacher-Masoch, who gave us the word *masochism*, is known to few, or less. This seems rather appropriate. While the Marquis de Sade strides around spanking Fame's bottom with a hardbacked copy of *The Hundred and Twenty Days of Sodom*, little Leo is forgotten in some ratty cellar, wearing a gimp-suit and whimpering over a copy of *Venus in Furs*.

Venus in Furs (1870) was Masoch's great work. It describes a chap called Severin who signs a contract with a lady (I use the term loosely) who is thereby:

> . . . entitled not only to punish her slave as she deems best, even for the slightest inadvertence or fault, but also is herewith given the right to torture him as the mood may seize her or merely for the sake of whiling away the time . . .

As you can imagine, *Venus in Furs* would make a splendid book-group read, or christening present. Yet even Masoch's masterwork is better known these days as a song by the Velvet Underground, whose lyrics have a fragile connection to the original novel, mainly in the use of the name Severin.

Venus in Furs was rather closely based upon Leo's own life. Masoch met a girl with the ridiculous name of Fanny Pistor. They signed just such a contract as the one above and set off to Florence together, with him pretending to be her servant. Exactly how much time Fanny Pistor whiled away and how is not recorded, and it's probably best not to try to imagine.

When, in 1883, Krafft-Ebing was casting around for a name for a newly classified perversion, he thought of Sacher-Masoch's novel. He wrote in *Psychopathia Sexualis* that:

> I feel justified in calling this sexual anomaly "Masoch-ism," because the author Sacher-Masoch frequently made this perversion, which up to his time was quite unknown to the scientific world as such, the substratum of his writings . . . he was a gifted writer, and as such would have achieved real greatness had he been actuated by normally sexual feelings.

Poor Leo was still alive when Krafft-Ebing appropriated his name for a psychological disorder. He was, apparently, peeved by the terminology. Mind you, he probably rather enjoyed the humiliation.

The Villains of the Language

History is written by victors. The Elizabethan poet Sir John Harington once wrote:

> Treason doth never prosper: what's the reason?
> Why, if it prosper, none dare call it Treason.

But history is a lot fairer than language. Language takes your name and applies it to whatever it likes. Sometimes, however, it *is* fair, as with the word *quisling*.

Vidkun Quisling was a Norwegian maths prodigy and invented his own religion. He also embarrassed himself rather during the Second World War by trying to get Norway to surrender to the Nazis so that he could be the puppet minister-president. He succeeded in his plan and ten weeks after his appointment *The Times* wrote:

> Major Quisling has added a new word to the English language. To writers, the word Quisling is a gift from the gods. If they had been ordered to invent a new word for traitor . . . they could hardly have hit upon a more brilliant combination of letters. Aurally it contrives to suggest something at once slippery and tortuous. Visually it has the supreme merit of beginning with a Q, which (with one august exception) has long seemed to the British mind to be a crooked, uncertain and slightly disreputable letter, suggestive of the questionable, the querulous,

the quavering of quaking quagmires and quivering quick-sands, of quibbles and quarrels, of queasiness, quackery, qualms and quilp.

And it serves him right. However, language isn't always on the side of justice. Consider these three names: Guillotine, Derrick and Jack Robinson. Which of those do you think was the nasty one?

Two Executioners and a Doctor

Once upon a time, hanging was the punishment for almost any crime. Even the great Elizabethan poet Ben Jonson, for the trivial offence of murder, was sentenced to death. The sentence was commuted when Jonson proved that he could read and thus got Benefit of the Clergy. Instead of being executed, he had a T branded on his thumb and was sent home with a warning.

The T stood for Tyburn, which is where the hangings used to take place. We even know the name of the man who would have hanged Ben Jonson: he was called Thomas Derrick.

Thomas Derrick was a nasty man. There hadn't been enough applicants for the role of executioner and so the Earl of Essex pardoned a rapist on condition that he would take on the job. That rapist was Derrick.

Derrick was a bad man and a good executioner. The two

are probably connected. In fact, Derrick was something of an innovator. Rather than just slinging the rope over the beam, he invented a complicated system of ropes and pulleys. He even, in 1601, executed the Earl of Essex, though being a noble, Essex was allowed the dubious honour of having his head chopped off, rather than hanging.

There's a moral in that, but I haven't the foggiest notion what it is—and the ethics get more complicated when you consider that Derrick's name survives and Essex's doesn't. The rope system he invented started to be used for loading and unloading goods down at the docks and that's why modern cranes still have a *derrick*. It's named after a rapist and executioner. There's no justice in this world: look at Jack Robinson.

There are three main theories on why things happen *before you can say Jack Robinson*. The first is that Robinson used to be the French term for an umbrella (because of *Robinson Crusoe*, in which the hero has an umbrella and very little else), and that French servants were usually called *Jacques*. This meant that when rich Frenchmen visited England and were surprised by the inevitable shower of rain, they would shout, "Jacques, robinson!" There is, though, no evidence for this theory at all.

The second theory is that there was an eccentric fellow in early nineteenth-century London who would walk out of parties without warning, often before you could even say his name, which was Jack Robinson. However, there's no contemporary evidence for this strange Jack Robinson's existence, so the second theory looks as dicey as the first.

The third and most plausible theory is that the phrase comes from Sir John Robinson, who definitely existed and was constable of the Tower of London from 1660 to 1679. He was therefore in charge of executions and was a stickler for efficiency rather than solemnity. The prisoner was marched out, put on the block and shortened without any opportunity for famous last words or blubbering. He didn't even have the time to appeal to the overseer of the execution. He was beheaded *before he could say Jack Robinson*.

So derricks and brief spans of time were both named after cruel and psychotic executioners. The guillotine, on the other hand, was named after a jolly nice chap.

Dr. Joseph-Ignace Guillotin had nothing whatsoever to do with the invention of the guillotine. In fact, so far as anybody can tell, he was against the death penalty. Nobody is sure who designed the first modern guillotine, but we know that it was built by a German harpsichord-maker called Tobias Schmidt.

It was Guillotin's kindness that got the machine named after him. You see, in pre-revolution France poor people were hanged, whereas nobles had the right to be beheaded, which was considered less painful (although it's uncertain how they worked that out). So when the poor of France rose in revolution, one of their key demands was the right to be decapitated.

Dr. Guillotin was on the committee for reforming executions. He decided that hanging was horrid and that axes were inefficient. However, a newfangled mechanism from Germany was, probably, the least painful and most humane method available. If there *had* to be executions, it was best that they were done with this new device. He recommended it.

In the debate that followed, on 1 December 1789, Dr. Guillotin made one silly remark: "Avec ma machine," he said, "je vous fais sauter la tête d'un coup-d'oeil, et vous ne souffrez point." ("With my machine, I cut off your head in the twinkling of an eye, and you never feel it.")

The Parisians loved this line. They thought it was hilarious. In fact, they composed a comic song about it. And thus Dr. Guillotin's name was attached to one of the most famous methods of execution. Thomas Derrick and Jack Robinson were both sadistic, heartless thugs, whose names live on in innocence, if not glory. Poor Dr. Guillotin's family were so embarrassed that they had to change their surname. There's no justice.

And sometimes with these eponymous inventions it can be hard to work out which came first, the word or the man. This is the case with Thomas Crapper, who invented the crapper.

Thomas Crapper

There's a myth that the word *crap* was coined for the sake of Thomas Crapper, the inventor of the flushing lavatory. There's also a myth that the word *crap* was *not* coined for Thomas Crapper. It actually depends on where you come from, and if that sounds odd, it's because *crap* is a sticky subject. Luckily, I have, as it were, immersed myself in it.

The first mistake that must be wiped away is that Thomas Crapper (1836–1910) was the inventor of the lavatory. He wasn't. The first flushing lavatory was invented by the Elizabethan poet Sir John Harington (who was quoted a couple of pages ago on the subject of treason).

Sir John installed his invention in his manor at Kelston, Somerset, where it's said that it was used by Queen Elizabeth herself. Harington was so pleased with the device that he wrote a book on the subject called *A New Discourse Upon a Stale Subject: The Metamorphosis of Ajax.* Ajax gets in there because in Elizabethan times the slang word for a privy was *a jakes.*

A whiff of the book's style and of the previous state of English crapping can be gained from the following extract:

> For when I found not onely in mine own poore confused cottage, but even in the goodliest and statliest pallaces of this realm, notwithstanding all our provisions of vaults, of sluces, of grates, of paines of poore folkes in sweeping and scouring, yet still this same whorson sawcie stinke, though he were commanded on paine of death not to come within the gates, yet would spite of our noses, even when we would gladliest have spared his company . . . Now because the most unavoidable of all

these things that keep such a stinking stirre, or such a stinke when they be stirred, is urine and ordure, that which we all carie about us (a good speculation to make us remember what we are and whither we must) therefore as I sayd before, many have devised remedies for this in times past . . . but yet (as the ape does his young ones) I thinke mine the properest of them all.

Americans like to talk about *going to the john*, and it has been suggested that this is in memory of John Harington. Unfortunately that's unlikely, as *john* in the lavatorial sense didn't appear until more than a hundred years after Harington's death. However, it *is* likely that *john* was an alteration of *jake*. Or perhaps we just like giving boys' names to the smelliest room in the house.

Harington's invention didn't catch on. Unless there are sewers and running water, a flushing lavatory is never really going to be viable for the mass market. It's like having an electric lamp without mains electricity, or skis without snow.

Sewers and running water arrived in Britain in the mid-nineteenth century, and what we generally think of as a lavatory was patented by Edward Jennings in 1852.

So who was Crapper? Thomas Crapper was born in Yorkshire in 1836. In 1853, a year *after* Jennings' patent, he came to London to start an apprenticeship as a plumber. He was jolly good at plumbing, and the 1850s were the golden age of the toilet trader. The new sewers meant that everyone could flush away their shame and smell. Business boomed.

Crapper set up his own company, Thomas Crapper & Co., and designed his own line of thrones. He invented the ballcock system for refilling, which stopped water being wasted, and added extra devices to stop anything unpleasant flowing back into the bowl after the flush. His were very superior lavatories, the pinnacle of plumbing.

Crapper lavatories were chosen for the residence of the Prince of Wales and for the plumbing of Westminster Abbey, where Crapper's name can be seen to this day on the manhole covers. The brand-name Crapper was everywhere, but *crap* had been around for a long time before.

All the dictionaries claim that *crap* first appeared in the 1840s, but, in fact, the word can be traced back to 1801 and a poem by a fellow called J. Churchill. Churchill's poem tells a story (which it claims is based on fact) about a subaltern in the army who feels the call of nature. He runs to the outhouse only to find that a major is already there, and as the major outranks him, he's forced to wait. The subaltern feels himself beginning to give way and his misery is compounded when a captain turns up and pulls rank:

Just adding (for some only mind number ONE)*
"I, I shall go in, when the major has done":
The Sub, who was, now, a most terrible plight, in;

---

*This is also the first-ever reference to *number one* in a lavatorial context. Most authorities have it down as a twentieth-century term.

And, not quite aware of priority S---ING,
Squeez'd awhile; "Well!" says he, "then, the best friends
   MUST PART";
Crap! Crap! 'twas a moist one! a right Brewer's ****!
And, finding it vain, to be stopping the lake;
"Zounds!" says he, "then, here goes man! I've brew'd; so,
   I'll bake."

That beautiful poem was written thirty-five years before Thomas Crapper was born, and half a century before he started plumbing. So *crap* is certainly not named after Crapper. Perhaps it was a case of nominative determinism. If you're unfortunate enough to be called Crapper, what are you going to do except work with it?

However, if Crapper didn't cause *crap*, he associated himself with it closely. All of his lavatories had Thomas Crapper & Co. written on them in florid writing and these lavatories were installed all over Britain. But in America, nobody had ever heard of either Crapper the man, or *crap* the word.

There isn't an American reference to *crap* all through the nineteenth century. In fact, there's nothing before the First World War. Then, in 1917, America declared war on Germany and sent 2.8 million men across the Atlantic, where they would have been exposed to the ubiquitous Thomas Crapper & Co. on every second lavatory.

It's only after the First World War that *crap, crapper, crapping around* and *crapping about* appear in the United States.

So it would seem that though the English word *crap* doesn't come from the man, the American one does. Crapper didn't invent it, but he spread the word.

Mythical Acronyms

Can you take another chapter on the same subject? Good, because we have something to clear up: *shit* and *fuck*, or more precisely, *SHIT* and *FUCK*.

You might have heard the story that both these words are acronyms. This is absolute twaddle.

The story goes that manure gives off methane. So far, so true. But then the story continues that when manure is transported on a ship, it needs to be stored right at the top of the boat to stop the methane building up to explosive levels in the cargo hold. So the words *Store High In Transit* used to be stamped on bags of manure before they were loaded onto a boat. *Store High In Transit* then got shortened to its initials—*S.H.I.T.*—and that was the start of *shit*.

It's an ingenious explanation and whoever thought it up at least deserves credit for imagination. Unfortunately it's absolute manure. *Shit* can be traced back to the Old English verb *scitan* (which meant exactly what it does today), and further back to Proto-Germanic *skit* (the Germans still say *scheisse*), and all the way to the Proto-Indo-European word (c. 4000 B.C.) *skhei*, which meant to *separate* or *divide*, presumably on the basis that you *separated* yourself from your faeces. *Shed* (as in *shed your skin*) comes from the same root, and so does *schism*.

An odd little aspect of this etymology is that when Proto-Indo-Europeans arrived in the Italian peninsula they used *skhei* to mean *separate* or *distinguish*. If you could tell two things apart then you *knew* them, and so the Latin word for *know* became *scire*. From that you got the Latin word *scientia*, which meant *knowledge*, and from that we got the word *science*. This means that *science* is, etymologically, *shit*. It also means that *knowing your shit*, etymologically, means that you're good at physics and chemistry.

Also, as *conscience* comes from the same root, the phrase *I don't give a shit* is thoroughly appropriate.

The other acronymic myth that we need to stamp out is that *fuck* is a legal term. The commonly believed myth runs that once upon a time, when sex could land you in jail, people could be taken to court and charged *For Unlawful Carnal Knowledge*. Nothing of the sort is true and there has never been such a term in English law.

The first recorded *fuckers* were actually monks. There was a monastery in the English city of Ely, and in an anonymous fifteenth-century poem somebody mentioned that the monks might have acquired some dirty habits. The poem is in a strange combination of Latin and English, but the lines with which we are concerned run thus:

Non sunt in celi
Qui fuccant wivys in Heli

Which seems to mean:

> They are not in heaven
> Who fuck wives in Ely

The modern spelling of *fuck* is first recorded in 1535, and this time it's bishops who are at it. According to a contemporary writer, bishops "may fuck their fill and be unmarried." In between those two there's a brief reference by the Master of Brasenose College, Oxford to a "fuckin Abbot." So it seems that the rules of celibacy weren't being taken too seriously in the medieval church.

Some scholars, though, trace the word *fuck* to even earlier roots. The etymologist Carl Buck claimed to have found a man from 1278 who rejoiced in the name *John Le Fucker*, but nobody since has been able to find the reference and some even suspect that Buck made it up as a joke. Also, even if John Le Fucker did ever exist, he was probably really *John Le Fulcher* or *John the Soldier*.

Acronyms are, I'm afraid, mainly myths. *Posh* does not mean *Port Out Starboard Home* and *wog* never stood for *Wily Oriental Gentleman*. There was a famous *cabal* formed of Clifford, Arlington, Buckingham, Ashley and Lauderdale, all conspiring against Charles II. But that was coincidence; the word had already been around for centuries.

But some acronyms do exist, just not where you might expect to find them. There's one hidden away in *The Sound of Music* that relates straight back to John the Baptist.

John the Baptist and *The Sound of Music*

About two thousand years ago a perfectly respectable lady called Elizabeth became pregnant and her husband lost his voice. He stayed silent as a silo until the child was born. The child was called John, and when John grew up he began telling people that they were naughty and chucking them in a river. Now, if you or I tried a stunt like that we'd be brought up by the police pretty sharpish. But John got away with it and, if you can believe it, was considered rather holy for all his attempted drownings. Chaps at the time called him John the Baptist.

Seven hundred years later somebody else lost his voice, or at least had a terribly sore throat. He was an Italian who went by the cumbersome moniker of Paul the Deacon, so he wrote a verse prayer to John the Baptist that ran thus:

Ut queant laxis
    resonare fibris
Mira gestorum
    famuli tuorum,
Solve polluti
    labii reatum,
Sancte Iohannes.

[O let your servants sing your wonders on,
With loosened voice and sinless lips, Saint John.]

69

Four hundred years after that, in the fourteenth century, somebody set this little poem to music. He (or maybe she) wrote a pretty, climbing melody, in which each line started a note higher than the last, until with the words *Sancte Iohannes* it dropped again to the bottom.

So the first note was on the syllable *Ut*, the second line began with the *re* in *resonare* on the note above, then *Mi* in *Mira, fa, So, la* . . .

The problem with *Ut*, though, is that it's a rather short syllable and difficult for a singer to hold. Try it. So *Ut* got changed to *Do* (perhaps for *Dominus*, but nobody's sure), and that gave *Do, re, Mi, fa, So, la* and, by extension, *Si* for *Sancte Iohannes*. Then somebody pointed out that there was already a *So* beginning with S and you couldn't rightly have two lines beginning with the same letter. So *Si* was changed to *Ti*.

Do re Mi fa So la Ti Do

Which is just a shortening of a hymn to John the Baptist. The shortening technique was invented by a fellow called Guido of Arezzo.

So *Do* is not a deer, a female deer, and *re* is not a drop of golden sun. The Von Trapp family were cruelly deceived.

Poor *Ut* was consigned to history, or nearly. It sort of survives. The lowest note was also known as *gamma*, after the Greek letter. So the lowest note of the scale was once known as *gamma* or *ut*. Then a whole scale came to be known as *gamma-ut*. And that's why when you go through the whole scale, you still run through the *gamut*. It all comes back to church music, rather like organised crime, which is, of course, crime played on a church organ.

Organic, Organised, Organs

Organic food is food grown in a church organ. Organised crime is crime committed by organists.

Well, etymologically speaking.

Once upon a time, the ancient Greeks had the word *organon*, which meant *something you work with*. An *organon* could be a tool, an implement, a musical instrument or a part of the body. For the moment, let's stick to the musical sense.

Originally, an *organ* was any musical instrument, and this was still the case when, in the ninth century, people decided that every church should have a *pipe organ* in it, for, as Dryden put it: "What human voice can reach the sacred organ's praise?"

Slowly the *pipe* part of *pipe organ* got dropped and other instruments ceased to be *organs* (except the *mouth organ*, which, if you think about it, sounds a bit rude). And that's why an organ is now only the musical instrument you have in a church.

Now let's return to the Greeks, because *organ* continued to mean *a thing you work with* and hence *a part of the body*, as in the old joke: "Why did Bach have twenty children? Because he had no stops on his organ."

A bunch of organs put together make up an *organism*, and things that are produced by organisms are therefore *organic*. In the twentieth century, when artificial fertilisers were strewn upon our not-green-enough fields, we started to distinguish between this method and *organic farming* and thus *organic food*.

The human body is beautifully and efficiently arranged (at least my body is). Each organ has a particular function. I have a hand to hold a glass, a mouth to drink with, a belly to fill, a liver to deal with the poison and so on and so forth. Heart, head, lungs, liver, kidney and colon: each performs a particular task, and the result, dear reader, is the glory that is I.

If you arrange a group of people and give each one a particular job, you are, metaphorically, making them act together like the *organs* of a body. You are *organising* them.

Thus an *organisation*: something in which each person, like each *organ* of the body, has a particular task. That shift in meaning happened in the sixteenth century when everybody liked metaphors about the *body politic*. However, crime didn't get organised until 1929 in Chicago, when Al Capone was running the mob (or *mobile vulgus* to give it its proper name—*mob* is only a shortening).

Clipping

When a phrase like *mobile vulgatus* or *mobile peasants* gets shortened to *mob*, linguists call it clipping. And there are more clips around than you might think:

Taxi cab = **Taxi**meter **cab**riolet
Fan = **Fan**atic
Bus = Voiture omni**bus**
Wilco = **Will co**mply
Van = Cara**van**
Sleuth = **Sleuth**hound (a kind of sniffer dog)
Butch = **Butch**er
Cute = A**cute**
Sperm whale = **Sperm**aceti **whale**
Film buff = Bu**ffalo**

Buffalo

How did *buffalo* come to mean *enthusiast*? What's the connection between the beast and the music *buff*?

To answer that, you first need to know that buffalo aren't buffalo; and also that *buffalo* is one of the most curious words in the English language.

The ancient Greek word *boubalos* was applied to some

sort of African antelope. Then *boubalos* was changed to *buffalo* and applied to various kinds of domesticated oxen. That's why you still have water buffalo (*Bubalus bubalis*). Any ox in Europe could once be called a buffalo.

Then the same thing happened to buffalos that had happened to turkeys. Explorers arrived in North America, saw some bison, and wrongly assumed that they were the same species as the European ox. Biologically they aren't related, and to this day scientists will become all tetchy if you call a bison a buffalo, but who cares? The name stuck.

Now, let's jump back across the Atlantic and take another look at those European oxen. They were called *buffalo*, but the name was often shortened to *buff*. European buffalo used to get killed and skinned and the leather that resulted was therefore known as *buff*, or *buffe leather*.

This leather was very useful for polishing, which is why we still *buff* things until they shine. When something has been properly buffed it looks good, and from that we get the idea that people who spend too much time at the gym running around like crazed gerbils are *buff*.

An odd thing about buff leather is that it's rather pale and, in fact, looks very like human skin. That's why naked people are referred to as being *in the buff*, because it looks as though they are dressed in buff leather.

Some people really did dress in buff leather, as it's a good strong material. For example, in the nineteenth century the uniform of the New York firefighters was made from buff and the firefighters themselves were often called *buffs*.

The firefighters of New York were heroes. Everybody loves a good conflagration, and whenever a New York building started burning the buffs would be called and crowds of New Yorkers would turn out to cheer them on. People would travel across the city just to see a good fire, and schoolboys would become aficionados of the buffs' techniques for putting them out. These devoted New York schoolboys became known as *buffs*. Thus the *New York Sun* said, in 1903, that:

> The *buffs* are men and boys whose love of fire, fire-fighting and firemen is a predominant characteristic.

And that's why to this day you have film *buffs* and music *buffs* and other such expert *buff*alos.

On the far side of New York state, beside the Niagara River, is a whole city called Buffalo, which is a bit odd as there aren't any bison there, and never have been. However, the Niagara River is very pretty, and the best guess about the origins of the city's name is that *Buffalo* is a corruption of the French *beau fleuve*, or *beautiful river*. But imagine if there *were* bison in the city of Buffalo. Pigeons in London are called London pigeons. Girls in California are called California girls. So any bison that you found in Buffalo would have to be called Buffalo buffalos.

Buffalos are big beasts and it's probably best not to get into an argument with one. That's why there's an American slang verb *to buffalo* meaning *to bully*. This means that if you bullied bison from that large city on the Niagara River, you would be *buffaloing Buffalo buffalos*.

But you can go further, and a linguist at the University of Buffalo did. He worked out that if bison from his native city, who were bullied by other bison from his native city, went and took their frustration out on still other bison from his native city, then:

> Buffalo buffalo Buffalo buffalo buffalo buffalo Buffalo buffalo.

Confused? The grammar is easier if you compare it to this version:

> Buffalo bison [whom] Buffalo bison bully [then] bully Buffalo bison.

It's the longest grammatically correct sentence in the English language that uses only one word. Word buffs love it.

Antanaclasis

Rhetorically, the sentence *Buffalo buffalo Buffalo buffalo buffalo buffalo Buffalo buffalo* is antanaclasic, which means that it keeps using the same word in different senses. People have been playing around with antanaclasis since language began. The Romans thought up the Latin sentence:

Malo malo malo malo.

Which means:

I would rather be in an apple tree than be a bad boy in trouble.

But neither the Romans nor the bison of Buffalo can come close to what you can achieve in Chinese if you really set your mind to it. Chinese is an incredibly tonally inflected language and you can change the meaning of a word by slightly changing the way you say it. When you add that advantage onto the principle behind *Buffalo buffalos* and *malo malo*, you can create something much longer. That's how a Chinese-American linguist came up with a poem that, in Westernised script, reads like this:

Shíshì shīshì Shī Shì, shì shī, shì shí shí shī.
Shì shíshí shì shì shì shī.
Shí shí, shì shí shī shì shì.
Shì shí, shì Shī Shì shì shì.
Shì shì shì shí shī, shì shī shì, shì shì shí shī shìshì.
Shì shí shì shí shī shī, shì shíshì.
Shíshì shī, Shì shī shì shì shíshì.
Shíshì shì, Shì shī shì shí shì shí shī.

Shí shí, shī shí shì shí shī, shí shí shí shī shī.
Shì shì shì shì.

Which means:

> In a stone den was a poet named Shi, who loved to eat
>   lions, and had decided to eat ten.
> He often went to the market to hunt for lions.
> At ten o'clock precisely, ten lions had just arrived at the
>   market.
> At that moment, Shi had just arrived at the market as
>   well.
> Seeing those lions, he shot them with his arrows.
> He brought the corpses of the ten lions to the stone
>   den.
> The stone den was wet, so he had his servant clean it.
> After the stone den was cleaned, he tried to eat those ten
>   lions.
> When he ate, he realised the corpses were really ten stone
>   lions.
> Try to explain this matter.

That's one hell of a case of antanaclasis. However, like the buffalo sentence, it makes no sense, even to the Chinese, unless it's explained.

China

Westerners find it terribly hard to pronounce Chinese words, and the Chinese find it hard to pronounce ours. In the nineteenth century when British merchants were over in China trying to trade opium, they found that the locals couldn't even say the word *business*, and instead pronounced it *pidgin*, which is why strange colonial dialects are still called *pidgin English*.

And we're so bad at pronouncing Chinese that when we want one of their phrases we don't adopt them as we would a French one, we just give in and translate. Do you have any idea how to pronounce *xi nao*? Luckily, you don't need to, as we translated it to *brainwashing* (it was originally a form of Buddhist meditation). We never lost face by trying to pronounce *tiu lien*; instead we took the phrase and translated it to *lose face*. As for Mao Tse Tung's *tsuh lao fu*, we call them *paper tigers*.

However, some Chinese words do get into the language, mostly because of the delicious food. These remain untranslated, which is generally a good thing. *Kumquats* and *dim sum* might sell more if English-speakers knew that they meant *golden orange* and *touch the heart*; however, *fish brine* would probably not sell as much as *ketchup*, *odds and ends* (basically leftovers) doesn't sound as exotic as *chop suey*, and nobody would eat *tofu* if they knew that it meant *rotten beans*.

However, as alien as the Chinese language may sound to Western ears, there are still some points where we can see that our languages connect, not because they are related (they aren't) but because humans form languages in the same way, for example by imitation of sound. That's why the Chinese word for *cat* is *miau*.

And here's a true oddity: the Chinese word for pay is *pei*.

Coincidences and Patterns

The Chinese for *pay* is *pei*, and the Farsi Iranian word for *bad* is *bad*. The Uzbek for *chop* is *chop*, and in the extinct Aboriginal language of Mbaram a *dog* was called a *dog*. The Mayan for *hole* is *hole* and the Korean for *many* is *mani*. When, in the mountains of the Hindu Kush, an Afghan wants to show you something, he will use the word *show*; and the ancient Aztecs used the Nahuatl word *huel* to mean *well*.

Any idiot can deduce from this that all the languages of the world are related. However, anyone of reasonable intelligence will realise that they are just a bunch of coincidences. There are a lot of words and a lot of languages, but there are a limited number of sounds. We're bound to coincide sometimes.

To prove that two languages are related you need to show a *pattern* of changes. It's not enough to say that the Latin word *collis* has a double L in it and so does *hill*. That wouldn't convince anyone of anything. But it's possible to show that hundreds of Latin words that begin with a hard C have German and English equivalents that begin with an H. Moreover, you discover that the rest of the consonants are pretty much unchanged. So the Latin *cornu* translates to Old German and English as *horn*. If you can show a pattern of changes, then you can be pretty damned sure that the languages are related. Let's give it a go.

So the English *horn of hounds* would be the *cornu canum* and the *horn of a hundred hounds* would be the *cornu centum canum* and the *hundred-headed hound with horns* would be *canis centum capitum cum cornibus*. And the . . .

Well, you get the idea.

The C to H shift that separates Latin from German is part of a group of shifts known as Grimm's Law, because they were set out by Jacob Grimm, who was one of the Brothers Grimm and who spent most of his time collecting fairy tales.

There are other parts to Grimm's Law; for example, Ps in Latin turn to Fs in German (and hence in many English words), which is how *paternal pisces* became *fatherly fishes*.

It's easy to see how this happens when you consider how it still goes on today. In the East End of London, people don't pronounce their Hs and haven't done so for at least a hundred years. The *house of a hundred hounds in Hackney* would be pronounced the *'ouse of an 'undred 'ounds in 'Acne*. Nor do East Enders pronounce the G at the end of participles, so instead of *humming and hawing*, a Londoner would find himself *'ummin' and 'awin'*.

The important thing is that people do this *consistently*. Nobody listens to *'ip hop*, or even *hip 'op*. You either pronounce your Hs or you don't. Once one H has gone, they all disappear.

Of course, East London English is still English, for now. But if somebody built a big wall around the East End and didn't let anyone in or out for a few hundred years, the captives would probably make more and more changes until their language became utterly incomprehensible to the rest of the English-speaking world.

Can that still happen?

Nobody is quite sure how transport and communication will affect the splitting of languages. On the face of it, you'd expect accents to stop developing as everybody adjusted to the tyranny of television, but that doesn't *appear* to be the case. In the U.S., for example, there's a thing called the Northern Cities Vowel Shift, whereby people in Detroit and Buffalo have started pronouncing *block* as *black* and *cot* as *cat*. That, in turn, has pushed the A sound, so that *cat* is pronounced as *cee-at*: so folks in Detroit would call the famous children's book *The Cee-at in the Hee-at*.

And accent changes are unpredictable. In Jamaica they don't drop their Hs, they pick them up. A Jamaican with a strong accent will *hadd han haitch honto hany* word that begins with a vowel. In New Zealand E has become I, so they have *six*. And though in Britain a *medal* is made of *metal*, in America a *medal* is usually made of a substance that's pronounced *medal*.

These laws are not absolutely consistent; but they're an awful lot better than you might expect. Also, words change their meaning and get shortened so you can't just take an English word, apply some transformations to it, and come out with perfect Italian. But all the European languages are closely enough related that for the basic words—like *father*, *eyes*, *heart*—there's probably a recognisable cousin.

This is particularly amazing when you consider how Europe has been overrun again and again by hordes of barbarians speaking barbarian languages like Frankish.

Frankly, My Dear Frankfurter

Once upon a terribly long time ago, there was a tribe called the Franks. They invaded Gaul and Gaul became *Franc*[k]*e*.

They oppressed the native Gauls horribly, forcing them to eat garlic and listen to Johnny Hallyday records. Only the Franks themselves were free. Thus they were en*franch*ised. They were able to speak freely, or *frankly*, and everybody else was disen*franch*ised and not able to approve things just by *frank*ing them.

How did the Franks get to France? Well, on the way they had to cross the River Main. This was easily done: they found a ford by which to ford it. The place became known as *Frank-ford on the Main*, or Frankfurt am Main.

Frankfurt is now best known as a financial centre, but it also gave its name to a kind of low-rent sausage called a *frankfurter*. By the same token, a *hamburger* comes from Hamburg and involves no *ham* (or in the case of many modern hamburgers, no detectable meat at all). Also, a *berliner* is a kind of doughnut from Berlin, which made JFK's famous remark—"Ich bin ein Berliner"—rather amusing to German audiences.

Back in ancient France the big export used to be incense, which therefore became known as *frankincense*, and at least one of the conquering Franks managed to cross the Atlantic still bearing his name of "Son of the south freeborn landowner," which translates to *Benjamin Franklin*.

You may notice a pattern here. Naturally, the Franks named good things like *frankincense* and *speaking frankly* after themselves. It's an absolute truth of linguistics that bad things are foreign.

Beastly Foreigners

The history of English prejudice is engraved in the English language.

These days the Dutch are considered inoffensive, charming even, but it hasn't always been so. The Dutch used to be a major naval and trading power just across the North Sea from Britain, and so Holland and Britain were natural and nautical enemies. Even when the two countries weren't fighting outright battles, the English would subtly undermine their enemies by inventing rude phrases.

Dutch courage is the courage found at the bottom of a bottle, and a *Dutch feast* is a meal where the host gets drunk before his guests. *Dutch comfort* is no comfort at all. A *Dutch wife* is simply a large pillow (or in gay slang something far more ingenious). A *Dutch reckoning* is a fraudulent price that is raised if you argue about it. A *Dutch widow* is a prostitute. A *Dutch uncle* is unpleasant and stern, and only tight-fisted diners insist on *going Dutch*. That'll show them.

In 1934 the Dutch government finally noticed all these phrases. They decided that it was too late to change the English language and instead made it a rule that their ambassadors in English-speaking countries only use the term *The Netherlands*.

The Dutch probably invented their own equivalent phrases about the English, but nobody knows what they are, as the Dutch language is *double Dutch* to us. Anyway, the English were too busy thinking up nasty phrases about their other neighbours.

Welsh rarebit used to be called *Welsh rabbit*, on the basis that when a Welshman promised you something nice to eat like rabbit, you were probably only going to get cheese on toast. The English also used to believe that the Welsh were crazy for cheese. *Grose's Dictionary of the Vulgar Tongue* (1811) records that:

The Welch are said to be so remarkably fond of cheese, that in cases of difficulty their midwives apply a piece of toasted cheese to the *janua vita* [gates of life] to attract and entice the young Taffy, who on smelling it makes most vigorous efforts to come forth.

By the same token, a *Welsh carpet* was a pattern painted, or stained, onto a brick floor; a *Welsh diamond* is a rock crystal; and a *Welsh comb* is your fingers.

When they had finished abusing the Welsh, the English phrase-makers turned their fury on the Irish, who made *Irish stew* out of leftovers. In fact, it was decided that the Irish were so nonsensical that nonsense itself was called *Irish*.

Yet the great enemy of England has always been France. We believed the French to be dishonest lechers, which is why a *French letter* is a condom and *French leave* is truancy, although here the French have got their own back by calling the same thing *filer à l'anglais*.

And when the English had got bored with just using the proper names of countries to insult them, they decided to think up nasty names for absolutely everybody.

Pejoratives

Here are some pejorative terms for the European nations and their origins.

Frog Short for *frog-eater* (1798). Previously (1652) the pejorative for a Dutchman because Holland is so marshy.

Kraut From the German for *cabbage*. First recorded in 1841, but popularised during the First World War.

Hun meant *destroyer of beauty* in 1806, long before it became the pejorative for German. That's because the Huns, like the Vandals, were a tribe who helped to bring down the Roman empire (the actual order was Vandal, Goth, Hun pushing each other from Germany through France to Spain and North Africa). Matthew Arnold called art-haters *Philistines* on the same basis of naming people you don't like after an ancient tribe. It was Kaiser Wilhelm II who first applied *Hun* to Germans in 1900 when he urged the army he was sending to China to mimic the behaviour of their supposed Hunnish forebears and "Take no prisoners," a phrase that's usually attributed to him, although someone had doubtless said something like it before ("I'll be back" is similarly attributed to the film *Terminator*). The word was taken up as a pejorative during the world wars as, though the Germans imagined their ancestors to be raffish and rugged, the British thought them beastly.

Wop (1912) American term, from Neapolitan dialect *guappo*, meaning *dandy* or *gigolo*.

Dago (1823) From *Diego* (obviously). Originally for either Spanish or Portuguese sailors.

Spic (1913) American term for anyone in the slightest bit Hispanic. Derives from "No *speak* English." Or maybe from *spaghetti* via *spiggoty* (1910).

However, language and history have been cruellest to the Slavs of Eastern Europe. Slavs such as the Bulgars spent many years battling against their neighbours. They weren't always successful. That there was a Byzantine emperor nicknamed Basil the Bulgar Slayer ought to give you some idea of what happened.

Basil the Bulgar Slayer once captured 15,000 Bulgars and blinded 99 percent of them. Every hundredth Bulgar was left with one eye so that he could lead his ninety-nine comrades home. Byzantine historians call this a clever tactic, but to our more modern minds it looks plain damned rude.

Basically, the Slavs had a hard time of it. When they weren't being slain by Basil in the south they were being subjugated by the Holy Roman Empire in the north and forced into lives of servitude. So many Slavs were defeated and oppressed that the word *Slav* itself became interchangeable with *forced labourer*, and that's where we got the word *slave*.

Now, before the next chapter, which common valediction surrenders you to a life of servitude: *adieu*, *toodle-pip* or *ciao*?

Ciao, Slave Driver

The word *slave* comes from *Slav*, and though it varies between Western languages the poor Slavs were everybody's original slave. The Dutch got *slaaf*, the Germans got *Sklav*, the Spanish got *esclavo* and the Italians got *schiavo*.

Medieval Italians were terribly serious fellows. They would wander around solemnly declaring to each other "I am your slave." However, being medieval Italians, what they actually said was *Sono vostro schiavo*.

Then they got lazy and shortened it to *schiavo*. In the north, where they were lazier still, this got changed to *ciao*.

Then, a few centuries later, the Italians got all energetic and tried to join in the Second World War. British and American troops were sent to tick them off.* These Allied troops picked up the word *ciao* and when they got back to their own countries they introduced it into English. It was considered a rather exotic new word. But be wary when you say *ciao*: however dashing and Mediterranean you may think you're being, you are, etymologically, declaring your own enslavement.

---

*This was a Good Thing, as the American troops were issued with rations of bacon and eggs. When an American GI was hungry he would pay a local chef to turn these basics into a pasta dish, and that's how spaghetti carbonara was invented. (At least, that's one theory, and there's certainly no record of carbonara before the Second World War.)

Ciao has an exact opposite, in the greeting *Hey, man*. In the United States, before the Civil War had finally established the idea that slavery isn't completely compatible with the Land of the Free, slave-owners used to call their slaves *boy*.

The Battle of Gettysburg freed the slaves and produced a memorable address, but it didn't, unfortunately, come with a socio-economic plan or a new language. Slave-owners weren't allowed to own slaves any more, but they continued to be rather nasty to their ex-slaves and kept calling them *boy* in a significant sort of way that annoyed the hell out of the manumitted.

All over America, infuriating white people would address black men with the words "Hey, boy." And it grated. It really grated.

That's why, in the 1940s, black Americans started taking the fight the other way and greeting each other with the words "Hey, *man*." The vocative was not inserted for the purposes of sexual identification; it was a reaction against all those years of being called *boy*.

It worked. White people were so confused by "Hey, man" that the sixties happened and everybody, of whatever race, started calling each other *man*, until the original significance was lost. This is an example of Progress.

Now, before the next link, are *robots* Martian slave-owners, Bolivian peasants or Czech serfs?

Robots

Once upon a time in the Austro-Hungarian empire, which ruled much of central Europe, there were lords and peasants. The lords owned all the land but peasants were granted portions of it to work for themselves. The peasant would then work his own little plot *and* the lord's. The bigger the peasant's plot, the longer he had to work the fields of the lord who had granted it to him.

This system, abolished by Emperor Josef II in 1848, was called *robot*.

The system was abolished, but the word, of course, survived. Seventy-two years later, in 1920, a Czech fellow called Karel Čapek was writing a play. It was a rather spooky, futuristic piece about a factory that produced willing servants out of biological matter. Mr. Čapek decided to use the Latin root *labor* (that gives us *labour*) and call these manufactured servants *labori*.

And that would have been that, were it not for Karel's brother, Josef, who suggested calling them *robots* instead. Karel took the suggestion and made the changes. The play was performed under the title *RUR: Rossum's Universal Robots* and was such a success that the word arrived in English two years later.

Of course, *robot* had cropped up in English before, but only in references to European politics that seem rather odd to the modern reader. Take this complaint of 1854 by an

Austrian aristocrat who believed that socialism has gone quite mad:

> I can get no labor, as the robot is abolished; and my tenants have now land of their own, which once was mine, to cultivate.

The English-speaking equivalent of *robot* was *indentured labour*, whereby a fellow signed a contract that made him a slave for a limited period. There are no extant records of indentured dentists, which is a shame because they both involve teeth.

In fact, lots of things involve teeth. Tri*dent*s have three teeth; *al dente* food is cooked for the teeth; and dandelions are *lions' teeth*, or *dents de lions* in French. But I digress. For the moment, we must stick to *indentations*, which are, etymologically, *bite marks*.

Medieval contract law was a sorry affair, largely because very few people could read. This meant that contracts could be signed left, right and centre, but few could tell which one was which. Most of us already have enough trouble finding some important piece of paper that we know we put somewhere safe; imagine how much harder it is for the illiterate.

There are two solutions to this problem, but as one of them involved learning to read, there was really only one solution, and it involved scissors.

A contract would be written out by a priest, signed or sealed by both parties (probably with an X) and then cut in half. This would not, though, be a straight cut. Instead, the contract would be cut up in a thoroughly wonky zigzag. Each party would then keep one half of the contract and, if they ever needed to prove whose it was, they would simply put the two pieces of paper together to show that the *indentations* matched. Thus indentured servants were indentured until the contract was terminated by a terminator.

Terminators and Prejudice

The *termination* is the end. That's because the Latin *terminus* meant *boundary* or *limit*, from which we get *bus terminals*, *terms and conditions*, *fixed-term parliaments* and indeed many *terms* for things (because a *term* has a *limited* meaning).

From that you get the idea of *terminating* somebody's employment. Legally speaking, you can do this in one of two ways: you can *terminate without prejudice*, meaning that you are open to the idea of re-employing the poor chap; or you can *terminate with prejudice*, meaning that you will never hire the scoundrel again. The latter is for employees who have done something awfully naughty and broken and betrayed your trust.

The CIA employs agents. If you break the CIA's trust and reveal their secrets to the Other Side, your employment will be terminated. Indeed, it will be terminated with prejudice. Indeed, the CIA often makes sure that nobody ever employs you again by the simple expedient of creeping up behind you and shooting you in the head. This they jokingly refer to as *termination with extreme prejudice*.

The CIA being awfully secret, it's hard to say exactly when the phrase *terminate with extreme prejudice* was invented. That it was revealed to the general public at all was the fault of the U.S. Army Special Forces: the Green Berets.

In 1969 a Vietnamese fellow called Thai Khac Chuyen was working as an agent or informer for the Green Berets (or possibly the CIA, or both). However, he was also working for the Viet Cong and when the Green Berets discovered this they became a little bit peeved.

They went (or didn't go, depending on whom you believe) to the CIA for advice on what to do about Chuyen. The CIA told the Green Berets to let bygones be bygones and to try to see it from the other chap's point of view, or at least that's what the CIA claim.

The Green Berets, on the other hand, say that the CIA told them that Chuyen (or his contract) should be *terminated with extreme prejudice*.

Exactly who said what is no longer of interest to Thai Khac Chuyen, as the upshot of the story is that he was shot. Eight Green Berets were arrested over the affair and, in the brouhaha and court martial that followed, the CIA joke about contract law was finally brought out into the open.

It was this incident that took the innocent word *terminate* away from contract law and bus depots and got it a part in the movies. First, there was a mention in *Apocalypse Now* (1979), where the hero is sent off to find Colonel Kurtz and *terminate* him *with extreme prejudice*. Soon, *terminate* was so sturdily established in the public mind as a big, tough, scary synonym for *kill* that in 1984 James Cameron decided to call his big, tough, scary killer-robot *The Terminator*.

Terminators and Equators

If you look up *terminator* in a dictionary, you're unlikely to find any reference to death or cyborgs. The first definition will be an astronomical one, because the terminator is the line that divides the illuminated part of a planet from the darker half. So the straight line down the middle of a half-moon is a terminator.

Astronomy and astrology (which were once the same thing) used to be big business until somebody pointed out that huge and distant balls of hydrogen were unlikely to affect your love life. Horoscopes were sent to skulk at the back of the newspaper with the crosswords and personals. Yet the terminology of astrology survives all over the language. For example, if a fellow is of a friendly *disposition*, it's because his friendliness is the inevitable consequence of the positions of the planets at the moment of his birth, or rather the distances between the planets, hence *disposition*.

If Jupiter was in the ascendant when you were born, you are of a *jovial disposition*; and if you're not jovial but miserable and *saturn*ine that's a disaster, because a *disaster* is a *dis-astro*, or *misplaced planet*. *Disaster* is Latin for *ill-starred*.

The fault, as Shakespeare put it, is not in our stars; but the language is.

Culmination, opposition, nadir, depression and *aspect* are all words that we have purloined from the horoscopes and telescopes of antiquity. However, astrology is not the only reason that the heavens take precedence over the Earth. There's the simpler question of visibility. The North Pole, for example, is very far away, and inconveniently located for public transport, but you can *see* the pole star from your house (providing you're in the northern hemisphere). The celestial equator is an imaginary projection of the Earth's equator out into space, and the stars through which this celestial equator passes shine brightly every night no matter where you are, although to reach the real equator requires a journey. And that's why the word *equator* referred to part of the sky two centuries before it referred to part of the globe.

Equality in Ecuador

Because the Earth wobbles on its axis, the celestial *equa*tor is over the terrestrial *equa*tor only twice a year, at the *equi*-noxes when night and day are of *equal* length. The Sun is a nomad and for the first half of the year it tramps slowly southwards until it gets to a latitude of 23 degrees, at which point it *turns* around and heads for 23 degrees north, where it *turns* again.

The Greek for *turn* was *tropos*, which is why a *turn of phrase* was for them a *rhetorical trope*. That's also the reason that the latitude of 23 degrees south is the *Tropic* of Capricorn and its northern equivalent is the *Tropic* of Cancer, and everywhere in between is *tropical*.

Bang in between the two tropics is the equator that runs like a 25,000-mile belt around the Earth.* The Spanish for *equator* is *ecuador*, so when they found a country through which the *ecuador* ran, they called it Ecuador.

The equator is called the equator because it divides the Earth into two equal sections, which therefore have *equality*. In most circumstances *inequality* is *iniquitous*, but sometimes iniquity is necessary. Not everybody can be equal. Take, for example, sport. You have two teams that have equal status, but when they argue you need somebody of higher status to judge between them. This referee is *not on a par* with them. In Latin he was a *non-par* and in Old French he was *a noumpere*, but then something happened to the N and he became *an umpire*.

An undignified fate often awaits words that begin with an N. Cooks used to wear a *napron*. But *naprons* were more often stained than written down, and so the A was able to

---

*In *A Midsummer Night's Dream*, Puck says that he will "put a girdle round about the earth/In forty minutes." This means that he must be able to travel at 37,000 miles an hour, or Mach 49.3

craftily steal the N away from *napron*, and now a cook wears *an apron*.

This fickle N is something to ponder next time you're bitten by *a nadder*, but I wouldn't ponder it for too long.

Sometimes the inconstant N travels the other way. What was once *an ewt* is now *a newt*; and an extra name, *an eke-name*, is now *a nickname*.

The Latin *par* also gave us *parity, peer groups, peerless* and *peers of the realm*. It may seem rather odd that aristocrats, who are above everybody else, should be called *peers*. The reason is that Charlemagne had twelve noble knights who were all equal, and therefore *peers*. In fact, Charlemagne didn't have twelve knights, but there was a *legend* that he did, and that's quite good enough for spawning a word.

Par hides all over the place. If you do somebody down and make them feel less important than you, you dis*par*age them; and if you have a girl to live with you as an equal she is an *au pair*. But the most obvious place that the word *par* survives is on the golf course, as the score between a birdie and a bogey.

Bogeys

Why is a score of one over par called a *bogey*?

Any game of golf is played against two opponents. You are competing against the other golfer and you are competing against the ground score, the scratch value, the *par*—the number of strokes a professional golfer should take to complete the course. Of your two opponents, the ground is usually the harder to beat.

There was a terribly popular song in Victorian England called "The Bogey Man." It was about the nasty mythical fellow who creeps into the rooms of naughty children and causes all sorts of trouble to all sorts of people. This song was running through the head of Dr. Thomas Brown as he played a round of golf in Great Yarmouth one day in 1890.

The idea of playing against the ground score in golf was quite new at the time. Originally, pars and eagles and birdies were unknown in golf. All you did was to add up your total number of shots, and whoever had the lowest was the winner.

This was the first time that Dr. Brown had played against the ground and he didn't like it. He preferred to play against an opponent because, as he observed, the ground always seemed to beat him. It was an enemy that followed him around the course but never appeared in person, and in the end Dr. Brown decided that his invisible opponent was the Bogey Man, just like in the song. His joke caught on in Great Yarmouth and then spread around the golfing world. The Bogey became a score.

Lone golfers were therefore playing against the Bogey and the word spread until it meant *par for the course*. It wasn't until the 1940s that the word shifted to mean *one over par*, and nobody is quite sure why.

Bugbears and Bedbugs

The previous story has an instructive little postscript. Within a few years, golfers had forgotten the origin of the word *bogey* and the par score for a course was blamed on a fictional golfer named Colonel Bogey. A book of golfing cartoons from 1897 contains the line: "I, Colonel Bogey, whose score is so uniform, and who generally win . . ."

This meant that in 1914, when Kenneth Alford wanted a name for his brand-new marching tune, he called it "Colonel Bogey" and thus *bogey* returned to the world of song whence it had sprung.

So who or what was the bogeyman? Bogeymen come in all shapes and sizes. Some are shaped just like bears. They live in the woods and they eat small boys who don't do as they're told. These are *bogey-bears*. However, the bogey-bear has diminished over the years. He has faded from his ursine grandeur, both in threat and in the length of the term. Nowadays a bogey-bear is a mere *bugbear*, and far from devouring a child whole, he is an insignificant annoyance.

Likewise, a *bugaboo* is now scoffed at by everyone except James Bond. James Bond is very careful about *bugaboos* and usually checks for them under his bed. Well, etymologically he does.

In the eighteenth century a *bugaboo* (which is of course a variant bogeyman) became thieves' slang for a sheriff's officer, or policeman. Nineteenth-century burglars were therefore scared of bugaboos or *bugs* for short. But they kept burgling anyway, and burglaries continued all the way into the twentieth century. Indeed, they were so common that people started to set up burglar alarms, and in the 1920s burglars began to call burglar alarms *bugs* on the basis that they acted like an automated policeman. If a solicitous homeowner had fitted an alarm within his house, the joint was said to be *bugged*.

From there it was one small step for the word *bug* before it was applied to tiny listening devices that could be placed inside telephones or teapots. And that's why James Bond checks his room for *bugs*, and that's also why there could actually be an etymological *bogeyman* hidden beneath your bed.

Bogeys and *bugs* have always been pretty much interchangeable. Myles Coverdale's 1535 translation of the Psalms renders the fifth verse of the 91st Psalm thus:

Thou shalt not need to be afrayed for eny bugges by nights.

Most subsequent Bibles have used the word *terrors*; Coverdale's is therefore known as *The Bug's Bible*. Then, in the mid-seventeenth century, *bug* mysteriously started to mean *insect*. Perhaps this was because insects are terrifying, or perhaps because they used to get into your bed like a bogeyman. The first six-legged bug on record was a *bedbug* in 1622. Since then, though, the word has expanded to mean any sort of creepy-crawly, including insects that crawl inside machines and mess up the workings.

There's a story that one of Thomas Edison's inventions kept going wrong. Edison couldn't work out why his machine kept breaking down, but break down it did. He checked all the parts and they worked. He checked the design and it was flawless. Then he went back to check the machine one last time and discovered the cause of the problem. A small insect was crawling around over his delicate electronics and messing everything up. This, so the story goes, is the origin of *bug* in the sense of a technical failing.

This story may not be completely true, but it's certainly the case that Thomas Edison was the first person to use *bug* in the technological sense. In 1878 he wrote in a letter that:

> It has been just so in all of my inventions. The first step is an intuition, and comes with a burst, then difficulties arise—this thing gives out and [it is] then that "Bugs"— as such little faults and difficulties are called—show themselves and months of intense watching, study and labor are requisite before commercial success or failure is certainly reached.

And in 1889, the *Pall Mall Gazette* reported that:

> Mr. Edison, I was informed, had been up the two previous nights discovering "a bug" in his phonograph—an expression for solving a difficulty, and implying that some imaginary insect has secreted itself inside and is causing all the trouble.

So the insect story *could* be true, or it could simply be that Edison was referring to *bogeyman* sprites that haunted his machines, working mischief in the mechanism.

Whatever the origin, the word *bug* caught on, and when your computer crashes due to a software *bug*, the fault lies with Thomas Edison and the bogeyman.

Von Munchausen's Computer

New things need new words, but they usually end up with old ones. Computers have been around since at least 1613, when being a *computer* was a skilled profession practised by mathematicians who worked in observatories adding up numbers.

When Charles Babbage invented the precursor of the modern computer he called it an *Analytical Engine*, and when his son improved on the design he called it a *Mill*, on the basis that mills were complicated technical things and that, like his new machine, they took stuff in at one end and spat different stuff out at the other. Then, in 1869, machines that could *compute* the sum of two numbers began to be called *computers*, and slowly, as those machines started to do more and more things, the word spread. When the first modern computer was officially christened ENIAC (Electronic Numeral Integrator And Computer) in 1946, it was already too late.

Early computers were simply calculators, hence the name. Then they got software, which had to be loaded up by the user. Then in the 50s, a method was invented whereby a computer would install its own software. The idea was that a single piece of code was loaded, which in turn would load up some more pieces of code, which would load more and more until the computer had . . . but first we must explain about Baron von Munchausen in the marsh.

Baron von Munchausen (1720–97) was a real person who had fought as a soldier in Russia. On his return home he told stories about his exploits that nobody believed. These included riding on a cannonball, taking a brief trip to the moon and escaping from a marsh by pulling himself out by his own hair. This latter feat is impossible, for the upward force on the Baron's hair would have been cancelled out by the downward force on his arm. It's a nice idea, though, and von Munchausen's preposterous principle was later taken up by Americans, but instead of talking about hair, the Americans started in the late nineteenth century to talk of pulling themselves up *by their own bootstraps*.

What's impossible in physics is possible in computing, and a computer that's able to load its own programs is, metaphorically, pulling itself up by its own bootstraps. In 1953 the process was called a *bootstrap*. By 1975 people had got bored with the *strap*, and from then on computers simply *booted up*.

SPAM (not spam)

In 1937 a new product came on to the American market. It was made primarily of pork and potato starch and was originally called *Hormel Spiced Ham* because it was made by Geo A. Hormel & Co. However, a vice president of Hormel had a brother who was an actor and presumably much better with words, and he suggested that it be shortened from *Spiced Ham* to *SPAM*. Another story says that *SPAM* may stand for *Shoulder of Pork And Ham*. Either way, the Hormel Foods Corporation insists to this day that it should be spelt with capital letters: SPAM, not spam.

Hitler made SPAM a great success. The Second World War caused food shortages in Britain, which caused strict rationing of fresh meat, which caused Britons to turn to tinned meat as it was less tightly rationed. The tinned meat to which the wartime Britons turned was SPAM, and this was shipped from America in gargantuan quantities. After the war, SPAM remained a staple of the British diet, especially in cheap cafés, which is where *Monty Python* comes in.

In 1970 *Monty Python* produced the SPAM sketch in which two people are lowered into a nasty café somewhere in Britain, where almost every dish contains SPAM. After a while, a group of Vikings who also happen to be in the café start singing a song to which the only words are:

SPAM
SPAM

SPAM

SPAM

SPAM

SPAM

SPAM

On and on and on *ad infinitum et nauseam*.

Monty Python is, for reasons best known to nobody, rather popular with computer programmers. There's even a programming language called *Python*, based on their sketches. This leads us, inevitably, to *Multi-User Dungeons*, or *MUDs*.

Multi-User Dungeons are not, as you might have imagined, strange basement rooms in the red light district. Instead they were an early form of internet game that existed in the 1980s. Clever computery fellows would use MUDs to show each other programs that they had written, but the most popular of these programs was a very simple practical joke.

The first command in the joke program was that the computer should print the word SPAM. The second command was to go back to the first command. The result was that the lyrics to the *Monty Python* song would be printed out as a screenful of SPAM. This would scroll down your screen forever and you couldn't stop it.

By 1990 SPAM had become programmers' slang for anything unwanted on the internet. When the *Monty Python* joke was continued on Usenet in the early 1990s the word *spam* gained wider currency. And that's why, when that Nigerian prince with all the Viagra and the saucy photographs of Britney Spears started sending his emails, they were called *spam*, or more properly *SPAM*; for you must remember that SPAM is a proprietary name, just like *heroin*.

Heroin

Once upon a time, cough medicines all contained morphine. This made people worried. You see, morphine is addictive, which meant that if you had a bad cold and took the cough medicine for too long, you might cure the cough but wind up physically dependent upon the remedy. The poor cougher of a hundred years ago was therefore faced with a choice: keep hacking away, or risk becoming a morphine addict. Many chose the cough.

So in 1898 a German pharmaceutical company called Bayer decided to develop an alternative. They got out their primitive pipettes and rude retorts, and worked out a new chemical: diacetylmorphine, which they marketed as a "non-addictive morphine substitute."

Like all new products it needed a brand name. *Diacetyl-morphine* was alright if you were a scientist, but it wasn't going to work at the counter of the drugstore. They needed a name that would *sell*, a name that would make people say: "Yes! I want to buy that product!"

So Bayer's marketing chaps set to work. They asked the people who had taken diacetylmorphine how it made them feel, and the response was unanimous: it made you feel great. Like a *hero*. So the marketing chaps decided to call their new product *heroin*. And guess what? It did sell.

Heroin remained a Bayer trademark until the First World War; but the "non-addictive" part turned out to be a little misguided.

And that's why heroines *are* connected to heroin. And it was all because people didn't want to be in thrall to morphine.

Morphing De Quincey and Shelley

Morpheus, from which *morphine* derives, was the Greek god of dreams. He was the son of Sleep and the brother of Fantasy, and he lived in a cave near the underworld where he would make dreams and then hang them upon a withered elm until they were ready to use.

Morpheus was the *shaper of dreams*—his name comes from the Greek *morphe* meaning *shape*. This is why, if you are *amorphous*, it doesn't mean that you're fresh out of *morphine*, but instead that you are *shapeless*.

Drugs and dreams are an easy association. If you smoke a pipe full of opium you will, like as not, fall asleep and have a *pipe dream*. The most famous consumer of opium was a nineteenth-century fellow called Thomas De Quincey, who wrote a memoir called *Confessions of an English Opium Eater*, which contains a wonderful and strange account of his drugged dreams:

I was stared at, hooted at, grinned at, chattered at, by monkeys, by paroquets, by cockatoos. I ran into pagodas, and was fixed for centuries at the summit, or in secret rooms; I was the idol; I was the priest; I was worshipped; I was sacrificed. I fled from the wrath of Brama through all the forests of Asia; Vishnu hated me; Seeva lay in wait for me. I came suddenly upon Isis and Osiris; I had done a deed, they said, which the ibis and the crocodile trembled at. Thousands of years I lived, and was buried in stone coffins, with mummies and sphinxes, in narrow chambers at the heart of eternal pyramids. I was kissed, with cancerous kisses, by crocodiles, and was laid, confounded with all unutterable abortions, amongst reeds and Nilotic mud.

De Quincey's opium dreams sound a little less than fun, and much of his biography is about his efforts to give up the drug. The book is much more moving than it is honest.

In fact, when De Quincey wrote his *Confessions*, he was simply out of cash and couldn't afford a fix. Luckily the book was so successful that he was able to maintain himself in top-drawer narcotics for the rest of his life. This life was surprisingly long. While near-contemporaries like Shelley, Keats and Byron fell out of boats, perished of consumption or died feverishly in Greece, De Quincey, drugged up to the eyeballs and beyond, survived them all by thirty-five years and died of a fever at the over-ripe age of seventy-four. He had been taking opium for fifty-five years.

During his long and meandering literary career, De Quincey was a master-inventor of words. His opium-fumigated brain was a mint where neologisms were coined at a remarkable rate. The *Oxford English Dictionary* attributes 159 words to him. Many of these, like *passiuncle* (a small passion), are forgotten; yet many survive.

Without De Quincey we would have no *subconscious*, no *entourages*, no *incubators*, no *interconnections*. We would be able neither to *intuit* nor to *reposition* things. He was *phenomenally* inventive, *earth-shatteringly* so. He even came up with the word *postnatal*, which has allowed people to be depressed ever since.

Antenatal had already been invented by the poet Percy Bysshe Shelley. Shelley wrote an (earth-shatteringly tedious) poem called "Prince Athenase." The story goes like this: basically, there's a prince and he's great and stuff, but like every second bloody hero of romantic poetry he's mysteriously sad. Nobody knows why.

Some said that he was mad, others believed

That memories of an antenatal life
Made this, where now he dwelt, a penal hell

Others believed that Shelley had talent, but needed a damned fine editor. Like De Quincey, when Shelley couldn't think of a word he just made one up. By the time he drowned at the age of 29 he had already come up with the words *spectral*, *anklet*, *optimistic* (in the sense of a hopeful disposition), and *heartless* (in the sense of cruel). He invented *bloodstain*, *expatriate*, *expressionless*, *interestingly*, *legionnaire*, *moonlit*, *sunlit*, *pedestrianize* (although not in our sense), *petty-minded*, *steamship*, *unattractive*, *undefeated*, *unfulfilling*, *unrecognized*, *wavelet* and *white-hot*.

He even invented the phrase *national anthem*.

Star-Spangled Drinking Songs

A *spangle* is, of course, a little spang: a *spang* being a *small, glittering ornament*. Therefore, to be *spangled* is to be *covered in small spangs*, a fate that befalls the best of us at times.

The word *spangled* crops up in a poem by Thomas Moore—not the famous one, you understand, but the nineteenth-century Irish poetaster. He wrote:

As late I sought the spangled bowers
To cull a wreath of matin flowers,

It was one of Moore's translations from the Greek poet Anacreon, who was an ancient boozer and lover and lyric poet.

Anacreon's poems (*anacreontics*) are all about getting drunk and making lyrical love in Greek groves. Anacreon was therefore a Good Thing.

Anacreon was, indeed, such a good thing that in the eighteenth century an English gentleman's club was founded in his memory. It was called the Anacreontic Society and was devoted to "wit, harmony and the god of wine." It was a very musical affair and two members wrote a society drinking song called "To Anacreon in Heav'n." John Stafford Smith wrote the tune and the society's president, Ralph Tomlinson, wrote the words. The first verse ran thus:

> To Anacreon in Heav'n, where he sat in full glee
> A few sons of harmony sent a petition,
> That he their inspirer and patron would be
> When this answer arrived from the jolly old Grecian
> "Voice, fiddle, and flute,
> No longer be mute,
> I'll lend you my name and inspire you to boot,
> And, besides, I'll instruct you like me to intwine
> The myrtle of Venus with Bacchus's vine."

Bacchus's vine is, of course, booze, and Venus was the goddess of sex. "To Anacreon in Heav'n" was a good song with a very catchy tune (which you know). Because it was hard to sing, it became an ad hoc test of drunkenness used by the police in the eighteenth century. If you could sing "To Anacreon in Heav'n" in tune you were sober and free to go. This is, if you think about it, an odd fate for a drinking song. It's also rather unfair to those who can't sing.

Unfortunately the song was so popular that it was usurped and stolen by a chap called Francis Scott Key, who wrote new words that weren't about drink, but about being able to see a flag flying after a bombardment.

Francis Scott Key was an American lawyer. During the war of 1812, he was sent to negotiate with the British fleet for the release of certain prisoners. He dined aboard HMS *Tonnant*, but when the time came for him to leave, the British got worried. Key was now familiar with the British battleships: if he went ashore he could and would pass all this information on to the American forces. This was problematic, as the British were planning to bombard Baltimore first thing in the morning, and if the Americans found out it would spoil the fun. So they insisted that Key remain on board, and he was forced to watch the bombardment from the wrong side (or the right side, if you're thinking about personal safety).

Bang went the guns, but the American flag at Baltimore remained high and visible amid the smoke. Key decided to write a song about it. He stole the tune from the Anacreontic Society, but wrote new words that went:

O, say can you see by the dawn's early light
What so proudly we hailed at the twilight's last gleaming,
Whose broad stripes and bright stars through the perilous
    fight,

> O'er the ramparts we watched were so gallantly streaming?
> And the rockets' red glare, the bombs bursting in air,
> Gave proof through the night that our flag was still
>   there;
> O, say does that star-spangled banner yet wave,
> O'er the land of the free and the home of the brave?

And the new title that he gave to an old drinking song takes us straight back to *small spangs*.

Torpedoes and Turtles

The conflict between the Royal Navy and the revolutionary Americans also gave us the word *torpedo*, which has nothing and everything to do with being *torpid*.

The Latin word for *tired* or *numb* was *torpidus*. From this we got the adjective *torpid*, which is still with us today. And that would be the end of the story were it not for electrical fish.

That there are electric eels is commonly known. But there are also kinds of ray that can produce electricity; in fact, they can produce 220 volts of the stuff, which is quite enough to knock you out, and therefore render you *torpid*.

In English they were once called *numb-fish* or *cramp-fish*, but the educated Latin name is *Torpediniformes*, with the major family being the *torpedoes*. As Lawrens Andrewe put it in his snappily titled book of 1520, *The noble lyfe & nature of man, Of bestes, serpentys, fowles & fisshes y be moste knowen*:

> Torpido is a fisshe, but who-so handeleth hym shal be lame & defe of lymmes that he shall fele no thyng.

For a long time, therefore, a torpedo was simply *something that rendered you incapable*. For example, there was an eighteenth-century dandy called Beau Nash who was awfully witty but had trouble writing well. "He used to call a pen his torpedo for whenever he grasped it, it numbed all his faculties." This is a shame, as Nash was meant to be the wittiest, most charming man of his day and when he died his wife went to live in a hollow tree near Warminster.*

But to return to the story: in 1776 the Americans were revolting. The British Navy sailed to New York, but so revolting were the Americans that the Brits decided to stay in the channel and blockade the harbour. The Americans didn't like this, and there was a fellow called Bushnell who invented a submarine with which to attack the blockading British boats in the most unsporting manner.

Bushnell couldn't decide what to call his new submarine: he seems to have been of two minds between the *American Turtle* and the *Torpedo*. In shape it resembled both. Eventually, he decided on the latter.

The idea of the submarine was that it had a "magazine or

---

*Yes, really.

powder" attached to it that it would screw to the hull of the British flagship. A timer would then be set, giving the submarine a few minutes to get clear, and then there would be a big explosion and the British boat would be blown to smithereens and beyond. This didn't happen, as the revolting Americans were foiled by the hulls of the British ships, which were copper-bottomed.

But the Americans were not to be deterred. Another inventor called Fulton took up where Bushnell left off (Bushnell for some reason ran away to the South and took on a new identity). Fulton worked to the same general plan, but he gave the name *torpedo* to the explosive device rather than the submarine itself. He also decided to change it a bit. Rather than the submarine getting right up to the enemy ship, it would instead fire a harpoon at it. The explosive device would be attached to the harpoon by a rope and contain within it a timer. So the submarine would pop up, harpoon the ship, and disappear before the charge went off.

Fulton's torpedoes didn't work either. Decades passed of utterly ineffective torpedo inventing and improvement. The torpedo was fitted with a motor and other such gizmos, but nothing was sunk with a vile torpedo until 1878, when a Russian ship torpedoed an Ottoman one.

And that's how *tired and numb* came to be a name for something *fast and explosive*.

Now, before the next story, what's the connection between Mount Vernon in Virginia, Portobello Road in London, and feeling groggy?

From Mount Vernon to Portobello Road with a Hangover

Relations between the Royal Navy and the Americans were, as we have seen, fraught. However, it was not always thus. The fault lies with George Washington.

But George had an elder half-brother and mentor called Lawrence Washington who had, in fact, been a British soldier. Specifically, he was a marine in the Royal Navy. As a recruit from the British dominions in North America, he served under Admiral Edward Vernon in the Caribbean, and was part of the force that seized a strategically important base called Guantánamo, which has some minor position in modern history.

Lawrence Washington was very attached to Admiral Vernon. So loyal was he that when he went home to the family estate, which had been called Little Hunting Creek Plantation, he decided to rename it *Mount Vernon*. So Washington's house was named after a British admiral.

Admiral Vernon's naming exploits didn't end there, though. In 1739 Vernon led the British assault on Porto Bello in what is now Panama. He had only six ships, but with lots of derring-do and British pluck, et cetera, he won a startling victory. In fact, so startling was the victory that a patriotic English farmer heard the news, dashed off to the countryside west of London, and built Portobello Farm in honour of the victory's startlingness. Green's Lane, which was nearby, soon became known as Portobello Lane and then Portobello

117

Road. And that's why the London market, now one of the largest antiques markets in the world, is called Portobello Market.

But Admiral Vernon's naming exploits didn't end there, either. When the seas were stormy he used to wear a thick coat made out of a coarse material called *grogram* (from the French *gros graine*). So his men nicknamed him *Old Grog*.

British sailors used to have a daily allowance of rum. In 1740, flushed from victory at Porto Bello and perhaps under the pernicious influence of Lawrence Washington, Vernon ordered that the rum be watered down. The resulting mixture, which eventually became standard for the whole navy, was also named after Vernon. It was called *grog*.

If you drank too much grog you became drunk or *groggy*, and the meaning has slowly shifted from there to the wages of gin: a hangover.

A Punch of Drinks

The etymology of alcohol is as unsteady as one would have suspected. For starters the word *alcohol* is Arabic. This may seem odd, given that Islam is a teetotal religion, but when the Arabs used the word *alcohol* they didn't mean the same stuff that we do. *Alcohol* comes from *al* (the) *kuhul*, which was a kind of makeup. Indeed, some ladies still use *kohl* to line their eyes.

As kohl is an extract and a dye, *alcohol* started to mean the *pure essence* of anything (there's a 1661 reference to *the alcohol of an ass's spleen*), but it wasn't until 1672 that somebody at the Royal Society had the bright idea of finding the pure essence of wine. What was it in wine that made you drunk? What was the *alcohol* of wine? Soon *wine-alcohol* (or *essence of wine*) became the only alcohol anybody could remember, and then in 1753 everybody got so drunk that *wine-alcohol* was shortened to *alcohol*.

Spirits arrived in the drinks cabinet by almost exactly the same root, but this time from alchemy. In *al*chemy (there's the Arabic *the* again) every chemical was thought to contain *vital spirits*, little fairies who lived in the substance and made it do funny things. On this basis gunpowder contained fiery spirits, acid contained biting spirits, and things like whisky and vodka contained the best spirits of all, the ones that got you plastered. It's odd that whisky and vodka get you drunk at all, as, according to their names, they are both water.

Vodka comes from the Russian *voda*, which means *water*, and indeed both words come from the same Proto-Indo-European root: *wodor*.

The word *whisky* is surprisingly recent. It's not recorded before 1715, when it leapt into the lexicon with the sterling sentence: "Whiskie shall put our brains in a rage." Philologists, though, are reasonably agreed that it comes from the Gaelic *uisge beatha* meaning *water of life*.

Why the *water of life*? The Scots hadn't made the name up, they merely took it from alchemical Latin. Alchemists, who were trying to turn base metal into gold, could find consolation for their failure in the fact that it's pretty damned easy to distil alcohol, which they called *ardent spirits* or *aqua vitae* (water of life).

It wasn't only drunken Scotsmen who took *aqua vitae* into their own language. The Scandinavians called their home-brew *aquavit*, without even bothering to translate, and the French called their brandy *eau de vie*.

However, the *water of life* is also a delightful euphemism for urine. This should be drunk in moderation. Morarji Desai, who was prime minister of India, used to start every day by drinking the liquor brewed in his own internal distillery, which he always referred to as "the water of life." Desai claimed that Gandhi had taught him the trick, although the Gandhi Institute denies this vehemently and says that Desai's story is balderdash.

Balderdash used to be a kind of drink as well. Not a very good kind of drink, mind you: it was wine mixed with beer or water or anything else that meant that you could sell it cheap. Balderdash was strange stuff, but not nearly so rum as rum.

Rum was once a thieves' word meaning *good*; but like most thieves' slang the adjective *rum* got a bad reputation and started to mean *queer* or *a little bit fishy*. It's hard to say which of these uses caused the Caribbean spirit previously known as *kill-devil* to be nicknamed *rumbullion*. Or perhaps it was just a variant of *rum booze*, in reference to rum's strong and sugary nature. It might even be something to do with the Devon dialect word *rumbullion* meaning *uproar*, or it could be the dnuora yaw rehto. Or maybe it was a *rum bouillon* or *strange brew*. Either way, *rum* is first recorded in 1654 and by 1683 people were already making *rum punch*.

Vodka, whisky, aquavit, balderdash and rum are just enough to make the sort of punch that will knock you out. Only just, mind you, because *punch* comes from the Hindi word for *five*: *panch*. That's because, technically, a punch should contain five different ingredients: spirits, water, lemon juice, sugar and spice. That's also the reason that the area of India that contains five rivers is called the Punjab.

Panch derives from the Sanskrit for five, *pancas*, which comes from the Proto-Indo-European *penkwe*, which went into Greek as *pent* and gave us a *pentagon*.

But if you want to get properly sloshed you need the queen of drinks: champagne.

The Scampering Champion of the Champagne Campaign

According to legend (the beautiful elder sister of truth), champagne was invented by a Benedictine monk called Dom Pérignon who shouted to his fellow monks: "Come quickly, I am tasting the stars."

This is, of course, balderdash. Making sparkling wine is simple; it's bottling it that was difficult. If you put fizzy wine in a normal bottle, it can't take the pressure and explodes. A champagne bottle has to contain six atmospheres of pressure.

Even now the caverns of Moët and Chandon lose every six-tieth bottle to explosion. Moreover, it was English glassmakers who perfected the method in order to keep their cider fizzy, and the French simply stole the technology to bottle their bubbly.

Champagne was originally just *vin de campagne*, or *wine from the countryside*. It was only in the eighteenth century that it came to refer to wine from the particular region around Épernay, where many of the worst bits of the First World War happened. That Champagne saw some of the worst trench warfare is no coincidence.

The German advance of 1914 started very well. They stormed across northern France with Teutonic efficiency, until they got to the champagne warehouses. There's something about finding the whole world's champagne supply that can make even a German commander find reasons for pausing, and the pause was all that the French and British needed. The Allies arrived, everybody dug trenches and the rest is War Poetry.

The German campaign took place during the summer. It had to. When winter arrives, armies generally have to find somewhere warm to hole up and wait for the snows and the gales to pass. Then in the spring they can set out into the *campagne* again, which is why an army fights a summer *campaign*: literally *on the countryside*.

Campagne comes from the Latin word *campus*, which meant *field*. The very best soldiers in the field were called the *campiones*, from which we get *champion*. So the champion of a champagne campaign would be the same thing three times over.

You can do a lot of things with a field. You can, for example, build a university on it, in which case you have a university *campus*. But what most campaigning armies do is simply take out their tents and guy-ropes and pitch *camp*.

Actually, there's another thing that armies usually do. Armies are mostly composed of men, young men, without any women to keep them company. This means that the soldiers have every reason in the world to try to sneak out of the camp to seek the solace of sex. Creeping out of camp was called *excampare* by the Romans and *escamper* by the French, but we call it *scampering*.

The ladies towards whom these young champions would be scampering were the *camp followers*, women of more enterprise than virtue, who would follow the soldiers around and rent their affections by the hour.

Camp followers aren't the classiest of broads (a *broad*, by the way, is a woman a*broad*). They tended to wear too much makeup to be truly ladylike, and their dresses were garish and their hair badly dyed. During the First World War, British soldiers started to call such a get-up *campy*. They also referred to such illicit sexual scamperings as *camp*. From here the word *camp* had to make only a short hop before it referred to a man in makeup (and maybe a dress) who had illicit sexual encounters, and that's why tarty men in makeup are, to this day, *camping it up*, often with a glass of pink champagne.

Camp, in the sense of battlefield, also wheedled its way

into German as *Kampf* meaning *battle*. So Hitler's book *Mein Kampf* could reasonably be described as rather *camp*.

Insulting Names

It's a funny thing, but Hitler wouldn't have called himself a Nazi. Indeed, he became quite offended when anyone did suggest he was a Nazi. He would have considered himself a National Socialist. *Nazi* is, and always has been, an insult.

Hitler was head of the catchily named *Nationalsozialistische Deutsche Arbeiterpartei* (National Socialist German Workers' Party). But, like the Cambridge University Netball Team, he hadn't thought through the name properly. You see, his opponents realised that you could shorten *Nationalsozialistische* to *Nazi*. Why would they do this? Because *Nazi* was already an (utterly unrelated) term of abuse. It had been for years.

Every culture has a butt for its jokes. Americans have the Polacks, the English have the Irish, and the Irish have people from Cork. The standard butt of German jokes at the beginning of the twentieth century were stupid Bavarian peasants. And just as Irish jokes always involve a man called Paddy, so Bavarian jokes always involved a peasant called Nazi. That's because Nazi was a shortening of the very common Bavarian name Ignatius.

This meant that Hitler's opponents had an open goal. He had a party filled with Bavarian hicks and the name of that party could be shortened to the standard joke name for hicks. (Incidentally, *hick* was formed in exactly the same way as *Nazi*. *Hick* was a rural shortening of *Richard* and became a byword for uneducated farmers.)

Imagine if a right-winger from Alabama started a campaign called **Red** *States for the* **Next America**. That's essentially what Hitler did.

Hitler and his fascists didn't know what to do about the derogatory nickname *Nazi*. At first they hated the word. Then, briefly, they tried to reclaim it, in roughly the way that some gay people try to reclaim old insults like *queer*. But once they got to power they adopted the much simpler approach of persecuting their opponents and forcing them to flee the country.

So refugees started turning up elsewhere complaining about the *Nazis*, and non-Germans of course assumed that this was the official name of the party. Meanwhile, all the Germans who remained in Germany obediently called them the *Nationalsozialistische Deutsche Arbeiterpartei*, at least when the police were listening. To this day, most of us happily go about believing that the Nazis called themselves *Nazis*, when, in fact, they would probably have beaten you up for saying the word.

So it all goes back to the popularity of the name Ignatius. The reason that Ignatius was such a common name in Bavaria is that Bavaria is largely Catholic and therefore very fond of

Saint Ignatius of Loyola, founder of the Society of Jesus, better known as the Jesuits.

The Jesuits were set up in the seventeenth century to combat the rise of Protestantism, which had become the state religion of England. They soon gained a reputation for being very clever indeed. But as the Jesuits' cleverness was largely directed against the Protestant English, English Protestants took their name, made an adjective—*Jesuitical*—and used it to describe something that's too clever by half, and that uses logical tricks at the expense of common sense.

This is a tad unfair on the poor Jesuits, who have been responsible for the educations of some of the most famous men in history: Fidel Castro, Bill Clinton, Charles de Gaulle, Cardinal Richelieu, Robert Altman, James Joyce, Tom Clancy, Molière, Arthur Conan Doyle, Bing Crosby, Freddie Mercury, René Descartes, Michel Foucault, Martin Heidegger, Alfred Hitchcock, Elmore Leonard, Spencer Tracy, Voltaire and Georges Lemaître.

And if the last name on that list is unfamiliar, it shouldn't be. Monsignor Georges Lemaître was one of the most important scientists of the twentieth century. His great idea, proposed in 1927, was the theory of the Primeval Atom, which of course you haven't heard of.

That's because the theory of the Primeval Atom, like the *Nationalsozialistische Deutsche Arbeiterpartei*, is a name that never made it. It vanished, usurped by an insult.

The theory of the Primeval Atom asserts that the universe has not been around for eternity, and that instead it started off 13.7 billion years ago with all matter contained in a single point: the Primeval Atom. This point exploded and expanded, space cooled, galaxies were formed, et cetera et cetera.

Many people disagreed with this theory, including the British astronomer Sir Fred Hoyle. He thought that the universe had always been around, and decided to undermine Lemaître's theory by calling it something silly. So he racked his brains and came up with the silliest name he could think of. He called it the *Big Bang Theory*, because he hoped that *Big Bang* captured the childishness and simplicity of the idea.

Names are not earned, they are given. Often the givers don't know what they're doing. Sometimes, it's simply a slip of a child's tongue.

Peter Pan

And sometimes names come out of almost nothing. W. E. Henley (the poet who wrote *Invictus* and not much else)* had a daughter named Margaret. Margaret died when she was only five years old, but not before she had met J. M. Barrie. She liked Mr. Barrie and tried to call him her *friendy*, but

---

*Thank God.

being only five and horribly ill, all she could make of the word was *wendy*.

J. M. Barrie then went off and wrote a play about a boy called Peter Pan who takes a girl and her two brothers off to Neverland. He named the heroine Wendy in memory of little Margaret Henley. So he gave her a sort of immortality, for the play was so popular that parents started to name their daughters after the central character. Although, why you would name your daughter after a girl who runs away from home with a strange boy the second the dog's not looking is a mystery.

Unfortunately, in *Peter Pan*, Wendy is shot with an arrow and dies. However, her death isn't a serious matter, as after a little bit of make-believe she recovers enough to start singing in her sleep. Her song is about how she wants a house, and so Peter and his associates build a tiny cottage around her dormant body. This was, of course, the first *Wendy House*.

Back in London, Mr. Darling, Wendy's father, is rather morose about the disappearance of his progeny. He realises that it's all his fault, as he had forced the family dog to sleep out in the kennel. So, as a penance, he takes to sleeping in the kennel himself. In fact, he never leaves the kennel at all and is transported to work in it every day. He is scrupulously polite and raises his hat to any lady who looks inside, but he remains *in the doghouse*. And so popular was *Peter Pan* that Mr. Darling's fate became a phrase.

So that's a name, a noun and a phrase: all from one story. But Barrie also took names that had been around already.

The most famous admirer of *Peter Pan* was Michael Jackson, a singer and composer of indeterminate tan, who named his home *Neverland*. This means that Mr. Jackson must have been working from the novelisation, because in the original play of *Peter Pan*, Peter doesn't live in *Neverland*, but in *Never Never Land*, a name that Barrie got from a thoroughly real place.

The very remotest and most unwelcoming parts of Australia, in Queensland and the Northern Territory, are known as *Never Never Land*, although today this is often shortened by Australians to *The Never Never*. Why give a place a name that refers to time? There have been various explanations for that.

It was claimed in 1908 that it was called *Never Never* because those who lived there *never never* wanted to leave, an explanation so remarkably unconvincing that it deserves a prize. An earlier and more plausible story comes from the *Gentleman's Magazine* of 1862:

> There is in a certain part of Australia a wide and desolate tract of land, a heart-breaking region which has been christened the "Never-Never" land. It is so called, I believe, from the impression which its drouthy wastes convey to the mind of the traveller on first emerging within its loveless limits that he will never again emerge therefrom.

But the actual origin is a little older and much more racial. A book of 1833 described the strangely peaceful wars of the local aborigines:

There is certainly more talking than fighting in their battles, and it is, therefore, to be hoped they will some day send over a few of their people as missionaries, to convince civilized nations that it is far worse to cut the throat of a man while alive, than to eat his body when dead.

I was greatly disappointed at not falling in with a tribe on Liverpool Plains, but the stockkeepers informed me that they had gone to war against the Never-never blacks, who are so called because they have hitherto kept aloof from the whites.

So Barrie's imaginary place came from part of Australia named after blacks who would *never never* have anything to do with white-skinned people. This origin is rather odd when you think about Michael Jackson.

Herbaceous Communication

At the time that the Never Never was being named, the British had decided that a warm, sunny country with beautiful beaches was clearly a great spot for a penal colony. If you were caught stealing a loaf of bread in early Victorian Britain you were sent to Australia, where there was less bread but much more sunshine. This system was abolished in 1850 when word got back to Britain that Australia was, in fact, a lovely place to live and therefore didn't count as a punishment. It was decided that lounging on the beach at Christmas did not produce what judges described as "a just measure of pain."

Rather than join the colony's work gangs, where they might be forced to do hard labour or, worse, administration, some of the more enterprising of the transportees set off into the Outback, where they obstinately continued to commit crimes. The Australian police would chase after them, hoping to arrest them and deport them somewhere else. However, the population at large tended to prefer the criminal bushrangers to the policemen, and would inform the furtive outlaws about exactly where the long arm of the law was reaching. This irritating and unofficial system of communication became known as the *bush telegraph*.

The *bush telegraph* isn't recorded until 1878, but that's because the telegraph wasn't introduced to Australia at all until 1853. In America, the telegraph had been around since 1844 and it took Americans only six years before they had invented their version of *bush telegraph*.

The *grapevine telegraph* became famous during the American Civil War, but nobody is sure who invented it or why. The Confederate soldiers seemed to think that they had invented the *grapevine* and that it was wonderfully Southern and lackadaisical. This view is backed up by a contemporary Yankee source claiming that:

> We used to call the rebel telegraphic lines "the grape-vine tele-graph," for their telegrams were generally circulated with the bottle after dinner.

However, the other story goes that it was the slaves of the South, those who picked the *grapes*, who were the true and original operators of the *grapevine telegraph*. In this alternative version, the grapevine telegraph was the sister system of the metaphorical *Underground Railroad* that took slaves from the South to freedom in the North.

Then, in 1876, Alexander Graham Bell patented the telephone, and the telegraph—bush, grapevine or otherwise—became old hat.* The telephone had a great effect on the English language. For one thing, it made the previously obscure greeting *hello* wildly popular. Before the telephone, people had wished each other *good mornings*, *days* and *nights*; but as the person on the other end of the line might not deserve a *good day*, people needed an alternative. Alexander Bell himself insisted on beginning a phone call with the bluff nautical term *ahoy*, but it didn't catch on and so *hello* rose to become the standard English greeting.

The other effect that the telephone had was that it made *telegraph* sound rather old-fashioned. So unofficial communication became known simply as the *grapevine*, which is

---

*A dictionary of 1776 defines "old hat" as "a woman's privities, because frequently felt."

why, in 1968, Marvin Gaye sang that he had heard dispiriting news of his beloved's plans *through the grapevine*.

Papa Was a *Saxum Volutum*

Marvin Gaye didn't write "I Heard It Through the Grapevine." It was written for him by Norman Whitfield and Barrett Strong, who also wrote the classic "Papa Was a Rollin' Stone," which is based on another old phrase.

Revolving minerals already had their (movable) place in the Rock and Roll Hall of Fame. Bob Dylan had written "Like A Rolling Stone" and some students from London had formed a band called The Rolling Stones, named after the Muddy Waters song "Rollin' Stone."

All these rock and rollers were referring indirectly to the fact that *a rolling stone gathers no moss*. This was observed in the 1530s by the poet Thomas Wyatt:

A spending hand that alway powreth owte
Had nede to have a bringer in as fast,
And on the stone that still doeth tourne abowte
There groweth no mosse: these proverbes yet do last.

The phrase also crops up in Erasmus' adages of 1500, where it's rendered in Latin as *saxum volutum non obducitur musco*.

But why are all these stones rolling? On the rare occasion that you actually see a stone rolling downhill, it usually gets to the bottom a few seconds later and stops. Its brief trip doesn't tend to knock much moss off, and if it does, then the moss will just grow back later. To keep a stone moss-free, it needs to be rolled *regularly*.

That's why the original rolling stones were not boulders crashing down a hillside. In fact, the sort of rolling stone that gathers no moss is helpfully pinned down in a dictionary of 1611 as a gardening implement used to make your lawn nice and flat. The solicitous gardener who rolls his lawn every weekend will find that his *rolling stone gathers no moss*.

Which means that Mick Jagger, Bob Dylan, Muddy Waters et al are all referring to diligent gardening. Moreover, one of the most successful bands of the twentieth century belongs in the garden shed.

The part of the phrase about *gathering no moss* actually predates the gardening implement. In the mid-fourteenth century you can find this observation on stone flooring:

Selden Moseþ þe Marbelston þat men ofte treden.

Which translates loosely as *moss doesn't grow on marble that gets trodden on a lot*. That line is from a mystic allegorical poem called *The Vision of Piers Plowman*. So before we proceed, what has Piers got to do with a parrot?

Flying Peters

Piers Plowman is a variant of *Peter Plowman* because the farmer in the poem was representative of the ideal disciple of Christ, the chief of the apostles and the first pope, whose real name was not, of course, Peter.

Once upon a time there was a fisherman called Simon. He fell in with a chap called Jesus who nicknamed him "The Rock" (presumably in preparation for a career in professional wrestling), which in Greek was *Petros*.

> And Jesus answered and said unto him, Blessed art thou, Simon Barjona . . . And I say also unto thee, That thou art Peter, and upon this rock I will build my church; and the gates of hell shall not prevail against it.

So Simon was—quite technically—*petrified*. And this Jesus chap, not content with renaming his friend, then decided to walk on water and, in contravention of every health and safety rule you can think of, encouraged Peter to do the same. This did not work out well.

> And in the fourth watch of the night Jesus went unto them, walking on the sea. And when the disciples saw him walking on the sea, they were troubled, saying, It is a spirit; and they cried out for fear. But straightway Jesus spake unto them, saying, Be of good cheer; it is I; be not afraid.

And Peter answered him and said, Lord, if it be thou, bid me come unto thee on the water. And he said, Come. And when Peter was come down out of the ship, he walked on the water, to go to Jesus. But when he saw the wind boisterous, he was afraid; and beginning to sink, he cried, saying, Lord, save me.

With that story in mind, what do you call a sea bird that appears just before a storm and dips its feet into the water? You call it a *storm peter*. And then you muck about with the letters a bit—just as a *cock* is a *cockerel*—until it's called a *storm petrel*.

Peter went into French as *Pierre*. *Little Peters* are called *Pierrots* and in French sparrows are, for some obscure French reason, therefore called *perots*. For reasons even more obscure, England then imported this word as *parrot*. The word first pops up in the alliterative claptrap that the Tudor writer John Skelton was pleased to call his poetry. Skelton wrote an attack on Cardinal Wolsey called "Speke, Parrot." Some fragments of the poem survive, which is a pity.

Parrot got verbed by Thomas Nashe at the end of the sixteenth century in the equally pointless but fantastically titled *Have With You To Saffron Walden*, an inexplicable work of incomprehensible invective.

Parrots are very important linguistically because they preserve the words of the dead. There was an explorer at the beginning of the nineteenth century called Alexander von Humboldt. He was in Venezuela and found an old parrot that still repeated words from the language of the Ature tribe. Nobody else did, because the Atures had been wiped out a few years before. Another tribe had slaughtered every last one of them and returned victorious with, among other things, a pet parrot. This parrot still spoke only words from the tribe that had raised him. So all that was left of a Venezuelan civilisation were the echoes and repetitions of a parrot.

Venezuela and Venus and Venice

The name *Venezuela* has nothing to do with *Venus*, but the chap who thought it up was related to her by marriage.

Amerigo Vespucci was a Florentine explorer with three claims to fame. First, and most obscurely, he was the cousin of a nobleman called Marco Vespucci. Marco married a girl called Simonetta Cataneo, who was possibly the most beautiful woman who ever lived. So beautiful was she, that even after she had died (in 1476) Botticelli still used his memory of her (and the myriad portraits that already existed) as the model for his "Birth of Venus."

But to return to Amerigo: not being as noble as his cousin, Amerigo was sent to work in a bank. However, the world of finance couldn't hold him and, at the invitation of the King of Portugal, he set off on an early expedition to the New World. On his return he wrote several accounts of his travels. These accounts were written in Latin and so he signed his name using the Latin form of Amerigo: *Americus.*

One of these accounts fell into the hands of a man called Martin Landseemuller, who, being a map-maker, ran off and made a map with the New World marked on it. He was going to call it *Americus*, but decided that ending a continent name with *–us* simply wouldn't do. *Africa*, *Asia* and *Europa* all ended with the feminine A, so he called it *America* instead.

Finally, Amerigo Vespucci named part of South America *Little Venice*, or in Spanish, *Venezuela*, because lots of the local tribesmen lived in huts that were built out into the water and supported by stilts, making it a sort of ramshackle miniature Venice.

What News on the Rialto?

For all its drainage problems, Venice has given the English language a fair number of words besides *terra firma*. Several parts of the city have entered the language. It was Venice that had the original *Ghetto* and the original *Arsenale*, where the warships were made. The first *regattas* were held on Venice's Grand Canal; and the lagoon in which Venice stands was the original *lagoon* (and is cognate with English *lake* and Scots *loch* and even the bibliographic *lacuna*).

Venice was the first modern democracy, which is why *ballot* comes from the Venetian word *ballotte*, which means *small balls*. Indeed, the word *ballot* arrived on English shores inside *The Historie of Italie* by William Thomas, because the Venetians would cast their votes by placing different coloured *ballotte* in a bag.

The same naming process happened with the voting in ancient Athens. When the Athenians wanted to banish somebody for not being classical enough, they would vote on the question by putting little black or white fragments of pottery in a box. White meant he could stay: black meant banishment. These tiles were called *ostrakons*. Hence *ostracism*. Ostracism has nothing to do with *ostriches* but is distantly related to *oysters* (both words relate to bone).

The method and term survives to this day in *blackballing*. In the gentlemen's clubs of London, an application for membership may be refused on the basis of a single black ball in the *ball*ot box.

In ancient Syracuse, votes for banishment didn't use shards of pottery. They used olive leaves and so ostracism was called *petalismos*, which is far more beautiful.

Venice was also the first place to introduce what we would now call newspapers. These appeared in the mid-sixteenth century and were little sheets describing trade, war, prices and all the other things that a Venetian merchant would need to know about. They were very cheap and were known as *a halfpennyworth of news* or, in the Venetian dialect, a *gazeta de la novita*. *Gazeta* was the name for a Venetian coin of very little value, so called because on it was a picture of a magpie or *gazeta*. *Gazette* was therefore a doubly appropriate name: it referred both to the cheapness of the news and to the fact that newspapers were, from the first, as unreliable as the chattering of a magpie, and filled with useless trinkets like the thieving magpie's nest. The Elizabethan linguist John Florio said that gazettes were "running reports, daily newes, idle intelligences, or flim flam tales that are daily written from Italie, namely from Rome and Venice."

How different from our own more modern magazines. Now, can you take a guess as to why a *magazine* is a glossy thing filled with news and a metal thing filled with bullets?

Magazines

Once upon a time there was an Arabic word *khazana* meaning *to store up*. From that they got *makhzan* meaning storehouse and its plural *makhazin*. That word sailed northwards across the Mediterranean (*the middle of the earth*) and became the Italian *magazzino*, which then proceeded by foot to France and became *magasin*, before jumping onto a ferry and getting into Britain as *magazine*, still retaining its original meaning of *storehouse*, usually military, hence the magazine in a gun. Then along came Edward Cave.

Edward Cave (1691–1754) wanted to print something periodically that would contain stuff on any subject that might be of interest to the educated of London, whether it be politics or gardening or the price of corn. He cast around for a name for his new idea and decided to call it *The Gentle-*

man's Magazine: or, Trader's Monthly Intelligencer. So far as anyone can tell (and in the absence of a séance we can only guess at Mr. Cave's thought process), he wanted to imply that the information in his publication would *arm* the gentleman intellectually, or perhaps he wanted to imply that it was a *storehouse* of information.

The first edition came out in January 1731. It was largely a digest of stories that appeared in other publications, but it also had its own column of amusing stories from around the world, such as the following:

> From *Dijon* in France, 'tis written that a Person having withdrawn himself, his Relations charg'd one who was his sworn Enemy with his murder, and examin'd him with such exquisite tortures that, to shorten them he confess'd the crime: whereupon he was broke alive, and two others as his accomplices were hanged. The Man supposed to be murder'd, soon after return'd home.

Or this pleasant round-up from the courts:

> This day one *Tim. Croneen* was, for the murder and robbery of Mr. *St. Leger* and his wife at *Bally volane*, sentenc'd to be hang'd 2 minutes, then his head to be cut off, his bowels to be taken out and thrown in his face; and his body divided in 4 quarters to be placed in 4 cross ways. He was servant to Mr. Leger, and committed the murder with the privity of Joan Condon the servant maid, who was sentenced to be burnt.

In fact, most of the first issue was taken up with stories of murders and executions,* and as the reading public has always loved a good bit of gore, *The Gentleman's Magazine: or, Trader's Monthly Intelligencer* was a big hit. But it was still a bit of a mouthful. So in December 1733 the *Monthly Intelligencer* part was dropped from the title and replaced with the slogan: *Containing more in Quantity, and greater variety, than any Book of the Kind and Price.*

But imagine if Cave had decided to drop the *magazine* bit instead: we might all now be buying *intelligencers.* Cave's caprice altered English. If it weren't for him, *porn mags* might now be called *carnal intelligencers* and that, I'm sure, would make the world a Better Place.

Moreover, Cave's *Magazine* gave employment to a young, penniless and unknown writer whose name was Dr. Samuel Johnson.

Dick Snary

It's absolutely necessary and fitting that a book such as this should devote a chapter to Samuel Johnson's dictionary. So we won't. After all, Johnson didn't write the first English

---

*I tried to count them all, but gave up.

dictionary. There were plenty before him and there have been plenty since. The chief recommendation of Johnson's is that he defines a cough as: "A convulsion of the lungs, vellicated by some sharp serosity."

Dictionaries had been around for ages before the Doctor. Johnson's dictionary was published in 1755 but the joke name *Richard Snary* was first recorded in 1627. Who was Richard Snary?

> A country lad, having been reproved for calling persons by their Christian names, being sent by his master to borrow a dictionary, thought to show his breeding by asking for a Richard Snary.

A word is always older than its pun. The word *dictionary* was invented by an Englishman called John of Garland in 1220. But it wasn't what we would call a dictionary; he had merely written a book to help you with your Latin *diction*.

The first dictionaries that we would recognise were dual-language ones for the use of translators. For example, the *Abecedarium Anglico Latinum* of 1552 is a terribly useful volume if you want to know that the Latin word for *wench always beaten about the shoulders* is *scapularis*. It also contains English words of indescribable beauty like *wamblecropt* (*afflicted with queasiness*) that have since vanished from the language.

The first dictionary that wasn't just there to help translators was Cawdrey's *Table Alphabetical* of 1604, which is a list of "hard usual English words" like *concruciate* (*to torment or vex together*), *deambulation* (*a walking abroad*), *querimonious* (*full of complaining and lamentation*), *spongeous* (*like a sponge*), and *boat* (*boat*).

However, the first English dictionary that actually had *dictionary* in the title was Henry Cockeram's *The English Dictionarie, or, An Interpreter of Hard English Words*, which hit the printing presses in 1623. Again, it's not complete, but it is useful. Before 1623 there were actually people who didn't know that an *acersecomicke* was *one whose haire was never cut*, or that an *adecastick* is *one that will doe just howsoever*. After 1623 they could look up such useful terms, and four years later Dick Snary was born.

Next up was Nathan Bailey's *Universal Etymological Dictionary* of 1721 that contained 40,000 words, which is only a couple of thousand short of Dr. Johnson's. The point of Johnson's dictionary is not that it was bigger or more accurate than the others (although it was slightly both); the point of Johnson's dictionary was that it was *Johnson's*. The most learned man in Britain had poured out his learnedness onto the page.

Suppose that you were an early eighteenth-century Englishman and you were arguing with a friend about the meaning of the word *indocility*. You pull out your copy of Nathan Bailey's *Universal Etymological Dictionary*, you flip through the pages and you find:

Indo'cibleness Indo'cilness Indoci'lity
[*indocilitas indocilité indocilità* (L.)]
unaptness to learn or be taught.

You sit back with a smug smile on your face, until your friend asks who this Nathan Bailey guy is anyway? "Well," you mumble, "he's a schoolmaster from Stepney."

Not that impressive.

But Doctor Johnson, on the other hand, was the foremost scholar of Britain. So his definition of indocility:

Indoci'lity n. s. [*indocilité*, Fr. *in* and *docility*.]
Unteachableness, refusal of instruction.

Well, that had the authority of Dr. Johnson behind it. It did not, though, stop Bailey's dictionary outselling Johnson's by a country mile.

Then came Noah Webster, who was an immensely boring man and can usefully be skipped; so that we can get straight on to the OED, which is the greatest dictionary ever. Nor is that opinion a case of anglocentric chauvinism, as the OED was largely the result of the collaboration between a Scotsman and an American. Its story also involves murder, prostitutes, and all sorts of other fun stuff. In fact, those of a weak disposition should skip the following chapter, as the story of the *Oxford English Dictionary* is too scary for most and will probably give you nightmares.

Still here? Right, for those who wish to continue, what is the medical term for slicing off your own penis, and how does it relate to the OED?

Autopeotomy

The *Oxford English Dictionary* is the greatest work of reference ever written, and it's largely the result of a Scotsman who left school at fourteen and a criminally insane American.

The Scotsman was a former cowherd called James Murray, who taught himself Latin, German, Italian, Ancient Greek, French, Anglo-Saxon, Russian, Tongan . . . well, nobody's quite sure how many languages he knew. It's usually estimated at twenty-five. Murray became a schoolteacher and then in the 1860s he moved to London for his wife's health and became a member of the Philological [*word-loving*] Society.

The Philological Society was trying to produce an English dictionary that would be more complete than any other. They eventually did a deal with the Oxford University Press, and James Murray, who at the time was still a teacher, became the editor.

The idea of the *Oxford English Dictionary* was that it would trace the development of every word in the English language. Each word would then have its meanings defined in chronological order with quotations given as evidence. Getting the quotations was a simple business; all that had to be done was to read every book ever written in English.

Even Murray couldn't do that alone, so he advertised for

volunteer readers,* people who would fight their way through all the books that could be found, copying out significant-looking sentences.

Now, let's leave Murray there for a moment and turn our attention to the island of Sri Lanka in 1834, where we will find a missionary couple from New England who are trying to convert the island's pagan population to Jesus. He is called Eastman Minor, she is called Lucy Minor and has just given birth to a son: William Minor.

The Minors were hyper-religious and at a very early age they decided that little William was much too interested in girls. Maybe they were just being Puritan and repressive, but given subsequent events it's possible that they were on to something.

Either way, the Minors decided that William's fascination with the opposite sex was a) a problem and b) probably something to do with the Sri Lankans. So they packed their son off to a boarding school back in the healthy cold shower that was nineteenth-century America.

There's no record of William Minor's sex life at boarding school, which is a blessed relief. All we know is that he ended up in Yale studying medicine, and that meant that when the American Civil War broke out he signed up in the Union Army as a field surgeon.

---

*Technically, the adverts went out before Murray was appointed, but we're trying to keep this simple.

Being a doctor is a pleasant business in general. You cure people and that makes them happy. Even if you don't cure them, they are still reasonably grateful that you tried. However, Minor was assigned the rather unhippocratic job of branding deserters.

If a chap got caught running away from the Union Army, he would have a big capital D branded on his cheek to inform everybody that he was a deserter and a coward. Minor was the man with the brand. At least one of the people he was forced to disfigure was an Irish immigrant, a fact that will be important later.

After the war, Minor was posted to New York, but he spent so much of his time in the company of prostitutes that the army got embarrassed and transferred him to Florida. It's a rather impressive feat to visit so many prostitutes that you become a scandal in New York. It's also an impressive feat to visit so many prostitutes that the army feels you're overdoing it. William Minor's parents may just have been right.

The next thing Minor did was to go utterly mad, and the army decided to discharge him completely. Minor moved to England to convalesce and settled in Lambeth in London, which was (coincidentally) full of prostitutes at the time. However, the prostitutes weren't the real problem. The real problem was the branding of the deserters, which still preyed on Minor's mind.

One day Minor met an Irishman called George Merret and, for no reason at all, decided that Merret was one of the men he had branded, on a mission of revenge. Minor took out a gun and shot Merret dead. This was unreasonable, as Merret didn't have a D burned onto his cheek. It was also, technically, illegal.

At the ensuing trial it was decided that William Minor was absolutely bloody crazy and he was confined in Broadmoor, the brand-new asylum for the criminally insane. Broadmoor wasn't actually that bad a place. It was a hospital, not a prison, and Minor was rich enough to afford a manservant and all the books he could read. It was at Broadmoor that he came across Murray's advertisement for volunteer readers.

Minor had a lot of time on his hands, and also the advantage of being criminally insane, which is always a plus in lexicography. So he started reading. He read and read and read and took note after note after note, and sent the notes to Murray. He sent Murray hundreds of notes, then he sent him thousands. Minor contributed so much to the *Oxford English Dictionary* that Murray would later say that the whole of the development of the modern English language, from Tudor times to the present day, could have been illustrated using only Minor's examples.

But Minor never said who he was. He seems to have been rather embarrassed about the murder, and Broadmoor Criminal Lunatic Asylum is hardly the most fashionable address in England. All Minor's letters to Murray were signed *W. C. Minor, Crowthorne, Berkshire*, which was technically true, as Crowthorne is the nearest town to Broadmoor.

It wasn't until the 1890s that James Murray discovered that his star contributor, the man on whom his dictionary was based, was an insane murderer. When Murray did find out, he immediately set off to visit Minor, and the two became firm friends. They were rather different people, but by coincidence they looked like brothers. They both had huge beards and flowing white hair, and they both loved words. Murray tried to give Minor emotional support but it didn't really work, as Minor, in 1902, deliberately sliced off his own penis.

This is called an *autopeotomy* and should not be attempted without due consideration. Minor did have a good reason. He had decided during his confinement that his parents and the army were right and that all his troubles came down to his excessive sexual appetite. Minor may have been correct, but most men intent on curbing their sex drive would have had the good sense to merely chop off their testicles (as the early Christian writer Origen did). The problem with an auto-peotomy is that, among other things, it becomes difficult to pee. William Minor was in trouble, and agony.

Murray took up Minor's case and in 1910 persuaded the home secretary to have Minor released and deported to America. Minor went back and died in his own country, but he took with him copies of the six volumes of the OED that had so far been completed. Whether these consoled him for the loss of his *membrum virile*, history does not record.

Now, who was the home secretary who released Minor, and what weapon did he help to name?

Water Closets for Russia

William Minor was released on the orders of the home secretary, Winston Churchill. Churchill is remembered by lexicographers as a man of words. He wrote a novel called *Savrola* that appeared in 1899 to reviews that can be given the usual euphemism of "mixed." He invented the phrases *out-tray*, *social security* and *V-sign*. He invented the words *seaplane*, *commando* and *undefendable*. He popularised *crunch* in the sense of *the vital moment*; and won the Nobel Prize for literature in 1953. With all these linguistic achievements, it's easy to forget that in his spare time Churchill was also a politician.

As William Minor sailed, sans willy, back to America, Europe was getting ready for war. In 1911, Winston Churchill was moved from the position of home secretary and became first lord of the admiralty, where he was in charge of developing new and more lethal methods of killing the enemy.

One of the ideas that he oversaw was the *landship*. The oceans of the world were, at the time, dominated by the Royal Navy. Britannia ruled the waves. Huge steam-powered gunships chuffed around the globe making sure that the Sun never set on the British empire. These ships were covered in iron, so that they were immune to enemy fire, and they had huge guns mounted on them, so that they could destroy others. However, on land Britain was not so invincible. The British army still consisted of men and horses, which are made of flesh rather than iron and could be killed in their millions.

So, under Churchill's supervision, a plan was hatched to

take the principle of the iron-clad warship and apply it to land warfare. The British started to design the *landship*. It would be iron, like a warship, it would motorised, like a warship, and it would have guns mounted on it, like a warship. It would be a destroyer, but it would be used in the field and not in the sea.

The idea was pushed forward by an officer called Ernest Swinton. Plans were drawn up and manufacturers approached, but everything was done in deadly secrecy. No mention of *landships* was ever made in public, which is why they aren't called *landships* today.

The landship was such a secret that not even the workers in the factory where they were built were to know what they were. By the outbreak of war in 1914, Russia was fighting on the Allied side, so Swinton decided that a good cover story for the new weapons would be to say on all documents that they were *Water Carriers for Russia*, but when Swinton told Churchill about his ruse Churchill burst out laughing.

Churchill pointed out that Water Carriers would be abbreviated to WCs and that people would think that they were manufacturing lavatories. So Swinton had a quick think and suggested changing the name to *Water Tanks for Russia*. Churchill could find no objection to this codename, and it stuck.

Well, it didn't all stick. *Water Tanks for Russia* was a bit cumbersome, so *water* got dropped. Then it turned out that the tanks weren't going to Russia at all. They were going to the trenches on the Western Front, so *Russia* got dropped too. And that's why tanks are called *tanks*. If Winston Churchill hadn't been so careful about lavatorial implications, they might have been called *carriers*. If Swinton hadn't been so careful, they would definitely have been called *landships*.

The tank was a very useful weapon of war, but unfortunately the Germans were even then building their own secret weapon, and theirs had a name that was quite ungentlemanly.

Fat Gunhilda

While Britain was developing the tank, Germany was building a gun. To be precise Germany was building an absolutely bloody enormous gun. It weighed 43 tons and could fire 1,800 pound shells 2½ miles. Its official name was the *L/12 42-cm Type M–Great Kurze Marine-Kanone*, but that's hardly the catchiest of names. So the designers at Krupp Armaments did a dastardly thing: they named it after their boss. The owner of the company was a fat woman called Bertha Krupp. So the engineers called their new gun *Dick Bertha*, which is German for *Fat Bertha*, or as it came to be known more alliteratively in English, *Big Bertha*.*

---

*Pity for Bertha Krupp would be misplaced. The Krupp *Berthawerk* was quite officially named after her, and that was the armaments factory attached to Auschwitz.

It's odd to give a cannon a girl's name. You hardly need to be a devoted disciple of Sigmund Freud to see a smidgen of phallic symbolism in a gun. However, history and Freud are at odds: for some reason guns are always girls.

During the Vietnam War, recruits into the U.S. Marine Corps were required to give their rifles girls' names, usually the name of their sweetheart at home; but the practice is much older than that. The standard issue flintlock musket of the British empire was called Brown Bess, and Rudyard Kipling joked that many men had been pierced to the heart by her charms. In Edinburgh castle there's a huge medieval cannon known as Mons Meg, which was probably named after James III of Scotland's wife, Margaret.

Why do guns have girls' names? It's a silly question because *gun* itself is a girl's name. So far as anybody can tell (and theories vary), the very first *gun* in history was a cannon in Windsor Castle. A document from the early fourteenth century mentions *Una magna balista de cornu quae vocatur Domina Gunilda*, which means "a large cannon from Cornwall which is called Queen Gunhilda."

Gunhilda is a girl's name and the usual shortening of Gunhilda is *Gunna*. So far as etymology can tell, every gun in the English-speaking world is named after that one *gunna* in Windsor Castle: the Queen Gunhilda.

There actually was a Queen Gunhilda as well. But what did she have to do with smartphones?

Queen Gunhilda and the Gadgets

Gunhilda was the Queen of Denmark in the late tenth and early eleventh century. She was married to Sven Forkbeard and, as is the way with Dark Age queens, that's all we really know about her. She was the mother of Canute the Great (he of the waves), and presumably she helped her husband out with his beard every morning. She must also have known her father-in-law, King Harald I of Denmark, who lived from 935 to 986 A.D.

King Harald had blue teeth. Or perhaps he had black teeth. Nobody's quite sure, as the meaning of *blau* has changed over the years. His other great achievement was to unite the warring provinces of Denmark and Norway under a single king (himself).

In 1996 a fellow called Jim Kardach developed a system that would allow mobile telephones to communicate with computers. After a hard day's engineering, Kardach relaxed by reading a historical novel called *The Longships* by Frans Gunnar Bengtsson. It's a book about Vikings and adventure and raping and pillaging and looting, and it's set during the reign of Harald Bluetooth.

Jim Kardach felt he was doing the king's work. By getting computers to talk to telephones and vice versa he was uniting the warring provinces of technology. So, just for his own amusement, he gave the project the working title of *Bluetooth*.

Bluetooth was never meant to be the actual name on the

package. Blue teeth aren't a pleasant image, and it was up to the marketing men at Kardach's company to come up with something better. The marketing men did come up with something much blander and more saleable: they were going to call the product *Pan*. Unfortunately, just as the new technology was about to be unveiled, they realised that *Pan* was already the trademark of another company. So, as time was tight and the product needed to be launched, they reluctantly went with Kardach's nickname. And that's why it's called Bluetooth technology.

Shell

The history of company names is strange and accidental and filled with twists and tergiversations. For example, why is the largest energy company in the world called Shell?*

Well, the truth is that in Victorian England seashells were popular. Really popular. Popular to an extent that just looks weird to us. Victorians collected seashells, painted seashells and made things out of seashells. The devouring dustbin of time thankfully means that most of us have never and

---

*Shell merged with Royal Dutch Petroleum to form the present Royal Dutch Shell.

will never see a whole imitation bouquet of flowers made of nothing other than painted integuments of mortal molluscs. The word *kitsch* doesn't do it justice.

These seashells had to be supplied by somebody. This is probably the reason that she sold seashells on the sea shore. But the beaches of Britain were not sufficient for the obsessed Victorians, so a lively trade started up importing bigger, shinier shells from all four corners of the Earth.

One man who cashed in on this importing business was Marcus Samuel, who set up shop in Houndsditch in east London and became a shell merchant. It was therefore perfectly natural that he should call his company Shell.

Shell did well and soon expanded into the other areas of the curio market: trinkets, brightly coloured pebbles and the like. Marcus Samuel brought his son (also called Marcus) into the family business and sent him off to Japan to buy gaudy trifles.

It was while on this trip that Marcus Samuel Junior realised that there might just possibly be a little bit of potential profit in, of all things, oil.

Shell did not remain true to its roots. The seashell business on which the company was founded was dropped.* Only the name survives, but the Shell logo that stands above

---

*In a spirit of scholarly enquiry, I tried to find out exactly when this line was discontinued, but the nice lady at Shell customer services thought I was making fun of her and hung up.

all those petrol stations is a mute memorial to what was once the core of the business, and to the fact that oil was only an afterthought.

In a Nutshell

Shells are strewn all over the beaches of the English language. Artillery, for example, can *shell* a town, on the basis that the earliest grenades looked a little like nuts in their shells. It's difficult to get a nut out of its shell, and it's also difficult to get money out of a debtor. That's why when you do manage it, you have made him *shell out*.

Hamlet said that he "could be bounded in a nutshell and count myself a king of infinite space, were it not that I have bad dreams," but that's not the origin of the phrase *in a nutshell*, which goes back to a deliciously unlikely story recounted by the Latin writer Pliny.

Pliny was a Roman encyclopaedist who tried to write down pretty much everything he'd ever heard. Some of his writings are an invaluable source of knowledge; others are pretty hard to believe. For example, Pliny claimed that there was a copy of *The Iliad* so small that it could fit inside a walnut shell. The weirdest thing about that story is that it's *probably* true.

In the early eighteenth century, the Bishop of Avranches in France decided to put Pliny to the test. He took a piece of paper that was 10½ inches by 8½ (this book is about 8 inches by 5), and started copying out *The Iliad* in the smallest handwriting he could manage. He didn't copy the whole thing, but he fitted eighty verses onto the first line and therefore worked out that, as *The Iliad* is 17,000 verses long, it would easily fit onto the piece of paper. He then folded the paper, sent for a walnut, and proved Pliny right, or at least feasible.*

The Iliad

The story of Troy (also called *Ilium*, hence *Iliad*) is magnificently grand. The heroes are more heroic than any that have fought since, the ladies are more beautiful and less chaste than all their successors and the gods themselves lounge around in the background. Winston Churchill once observed that William Gladstone "read Homer for fun, which I thought served him right."

However, Homer's words are not nearly as grand as they ought to be. If Ajax—the giant, musclebound hero of the Greeks—had known that he would end up as a popular cleaning product, he might have committed suicide earlier. Hector, the proud hero of the Trojans who would challenge

---

*A similar feat was, apparently, achieved in about 1590 by an Englishman called Peter Bales, who did it with the Bible.

anyone, even Achilles, to a fight, has ended up as a verb, *to hector*, meaning little more than *to annoy with abusive shouting*.

Hector's sister, Cassandra, is now a byword for a moaning, doom-mongering party pooper. Even the great Trojan horse is now a rather irritating kind of computer virus, designed to steal your credit card details and Facebook log-in.

And the phrases? There are very few famous phrases from *The Iliad*. There are a lot of famous lines *about* Troy:

> Is this the face that launched a thousand ships
> And burnt the topless towers of Ilium?
> Sweet Helen, make me immortal with a kiss.

But this is from Marlowe, not Homer. In fact, the only phrase that could be ascribed to Homer that most people know comes from William Cullen Bryant's 1878 translation, where Agamemnon prays that he'll be able to kill Hector:

> May his fellow warriors, many a one,
> Fall round him to the earth and bite the dust.

Would Homer be proud that his only memorable line was a middling song by Queen?

And the most famous phrase from the most famous Homeric hero isn't Homer's at all. It wasn't until more than two millennia after Homer's death that people started to talk about the *Achilles tendon*. The myth runs that, because of his mother's magic, the only part of Achilles' body that could be wounded was the back of his ankle, hence the expression *Achilles' heel* and the medical term *Achilles' tendon*.

The Trojan War, if it happened at all, happened in about 1250 B.C., Homer, if he/she existed, probably scribbled his way to immortality in the eighth century before Jesus. Philip Verheyen wasn't born until 1648 in the unfortunately named Belgian town of Borring, and it was Philip Verheyen who named the Achilles tendon, in the most unfortunate of circumstances.

Verheyen was a very intelligent boy who started out as a cowherd (like the editor of the *Oxford English Dictionary*), but became an anatomist. Verheyen was one of the great dissectors, so when his own leg had to be amputated, it was partly a tragedy and partly a temptation.

Verheyen was an ardent Christian who believed in the physical resurrection of the body. He therefore did not want his leg to be buried separately from the rest of him, as this would be a great inconvenience at the Day of Judgement. So he preserved it using chemicals, kept it with him at all times and after a few years began to very carefully dissect his own leg.

Carefully cutting up your own body is probably not good for the sanity. Verheyen started writing letters to his own leg, in which he recorded all his new findings. It's in these letters to a limb that we first find the term *chorda Achillis*, or *Achilles tendon*.

Verheyen went mad before he died. A student of his recounted visiting him in the last year of his life. Verheyen was gazing out of the window of his study. Beside him, on a table, was every last tiny piece of his leg laid out and neatly labelled.

The Human Body

The body, by virtue of proximity, is the source of at least a thousand and one words and phrases. There's barely a part of you left that hasn't been made into some sort of verb. Most, like *heading off*, or *stomaching criticism*, are obvious. Some are less so. *Footing the bill*, for example, is a strange phrase until you remember basic arithmetic. You compile a bill by writing down the various charges in a column and then working out the total, which you write at the *foot* of the column. At this point you may find that you are paying *through the nose*, which seems to be a reference to the pain of a nosebleed.

There are phrases based on parts of the body that you probably didn't know you had. The *heart strings*, for example, upon which people so often play and tug are actual and vital parts of your heart. The medical name for them is the *chordae tendineae*, and if anyone ever actually pulled on them it would at least cause an arrhythmia and probably kill you.

There are words that don't appear to have anything to do with the body but do, like *window*, which was originally a *wind-eye*, because, though you can look out through it like an eye, in the days before glass the wind could get in.

There's more in your eye than meets the eye. For a start,

there are apples. Early anatomists thought that the centre of the eye was a solid that appeared to be shaped like an apple, hence the *apple of your eye*. These days it has an even stranger name. It's called a *pupil*. And, yes, that's the same sort of pupil you have in a school.

In Latin a little boy was called a *pupus* and a little girl was called a *pupa* (which is also where we get *pupae* for baby insects). When they went to school they became school *pupils*. Now gaze deeply into somebody's eyes. Anyone will do. What do you see? You ought to see a tiny reflection of yourself gazing back. This little version of you seems like a child, and that's why it's a *pupil*.

But the part of your body that has the most words named after it is the hand.

The Five Fingers

And there was yet a battle in Gath, where was a man of great stature, that had on every hand six fingers, and on every foot six toes, four and twenty in number.

2 Samuel XXI, v. 20

Human beings count in tens. We say twenty-one, two, three et cetera until we get to twenty-nine, thirty. Then we start again with thirty-one, two, three, four until we get to another multiple of ten and the process repeats. The reason we do this is that we have five fingers on each hand, making ten in total. If the three-fingered sloth could count, he would probably do so in groups of six.

Counting on your fingers is such a natural thing to do that the word *digit*, which originally just meant *finger*, now means *number* as well. This also means that when information is stored in the form of numbers it becomes *digital*.

The Old English names for the fingers were much more fun than our own. The *index finger* was once the *towcher*, or *toucher*, because it was used for *touching* things. We call it the index finger, but not because we use it for running through the index of a book. Both *indexes* come from the Latin word *indicare* because an index, whether it's in a book or on your hand, can *indicate* or point you in the right direction. It's the *pointing* finger.

The boringly named *middle finger* was once called the *fool's finger*. The Romans called it *digitus infamis* (*infamous*), *obscenus* (*obscene*) and *impudicus* (*rude*). This is because they invented the habit of sticking the middle finger up at people they didn't like. The Roman poet Martial once wrote an epigram that went:

> Rideto multum qui te, Sextille, cinaedum
> dixerit et digitum porrigito medium

Which translates *extraordinarily* loosely as:

> If you are called a poof don't pause or linger
> But laugh and show the chap your middle finger.

The fourth finger has a strange anatomical property that gives it both its ancient and modern names: the *leech finger* and the *ring finger*.

There is a vein that runs directly from the fourth finger to the heart, or at least that's what doctors used to believe. Nobody is quite sure why, as there isn't actually any such thing. Yet it was this belief that made the fourth finger vital in medieval medicine. Doctors reasoned that if this finger connected directly to the heart, then it was probably possible to use it as a proxy. You could cure heart disease and treat heart attacks simply by doing things to the fourth finger of the patient's hand. The medieval word for a doctor was a *leech*,* and so this digit used to be known as the *leech finger*.

Who would be so silly as to believe anything like that nowadays? Well, anybody who's married. You see, we put the wedding ring on that finger precisely because of that non-existent vein. If the finger and the heart are that closely connected, then you can trap your lover's heart simply by encircling the finger in a gold ring. Hence *ring finger*.

And the little finger? Well the Old English used to use that for scratching their ears, and so they called it the *ear finger*.

---

*Contrary to popular belief, this probably has nothing to do with their sticking leeches on their patients.

Hoax Bodies

Let us finish our tour of the human body with the Latin word for the whole thing: *corpus*. It's pretty obvious how this word gave us *corpse* and *corporal* punishment. It's a lot less obvious how it gave us words for magic and fraud. To explain that we'll have to go back to a certain supper that took place in Jerusalem in around 33 A.D.

> And as they were eating, Jesus took bread, and blessed it, and brake it, and gave it to the disciples, and said, Take, eat; this is my body.
>
> Matthew XXVI, v. 26

Funny chap, Jesus. First, it's a little strange to assert that a piece of bread is your body. If you or I tried that we wouldn't be believed. We certainly wouldn't be allowed to run a bakery. Yet, given that Jesus was the son of God,* we'll just have to take him at his word.

What's odd is the cannibalistic non sequitur. If Jesus had said, "Take, eat; this is plain old bread and not human flesh," then the sentence would make sense. As it is, Jesus tells his disciples, "This is not bread, this is human flesh.

---

*This point has occasionally been disputed by people who will burn forever in God's loving torment.

What's more, it's my flesh. Now eat it up like good little cannibals."

It's enough to make you curious.

Christianity's cannibalism is something so central to Western culture that it often escapes our notice. During the crusades, the Muslims got rather worried about it. Nobody was sure how far the Christian's cannibalism went, and rumours spread around the Near East of Muslims being cooked and eaten. When the Christians tried to explain that they only ate God, they just seemed to be adding blasphemy to their sins.

You were meant to take the cannibalism literally, as well. At the time, a Christian could be burnt at the stake for denying the literal truth of transubstantiation. The communion wafer was *actually* turned into Jesus' flesh. All that remained of the original wafer were what theologians called the *accidentals*. The accidentals were those qualities that meant that the wafer still looked, smelled, felt and tasted like a wafer. Other than that it was wholly transformed.

This change was effected by the priest taking the wafer and saying the magic words: "*Hoc est corpus meum*: this is my body."

And then in the sixteenth century Protestantism happened. This new form of Christianity asserted, among other things, that the wafer did *not* turn into Jesus' flesh but merely represented it.

Rather than behaving like gentlemen and agreeing to differ, the Protestants and Catholics got into an awful spat about whether the wafer was or wasn't the Lord's flesh, and did all sorts of things like burning each other, attaching each other to racks and making jokes at each other's expense.

In the court of the Protestant King James I, there was a clown who used to perform comical magic tricks, during which he would intone the cod-magical words: *Hocus Pocus*. Indeed, the clown called himself *His Majesty's Most Excellent Hocus Pocus*, and the phrase caught on. Where did it come from?

> In all probability [says a seventeenth-century sermon] those common juggling words of *hocus pocus* are nothing else but a corruption of *hoc est corpus*, by way of ridiculous imitation of the priests of the Church of Rome in their trick of Transubstantiation.

From the body to cannibalism to religion to magic: *corpus* has come a long way, but it still has a long way to go. *Hocus pocus* got shortened to *hoax*.

The words of Jesus had been translated, parodied, shortened, and now they meant an outright, barefaced con. And it didn't stop there. *Hoax* got changed again: not shortened this time, but lengthened. *Hoax* became *hokum*, an American phrase meaning *nonsense* or *rubbish* or *bunkum*. In fact, it probably gained its *–kum* in order to make it sound more like *bunkum*.

Now, does *bunkum* relate to *bunk beds*, *golfing bunkers*, or *reedy valleys*?

Bunking and Debunking

It's awfully tempting to think that *debunking* has something to do with bunk beds. One imagines that a false idea is found snoozing under a duvet, is woken up and thrown out of his bunk bed by big, burly reason. This is, alas, nonsense.

Debunking is the process of getting rid of an idea that is *bunk* or *bunkum*. *Bunkum*, as we all know, is complete and utter nonsense, but it's also a place in North Carolina. Buncombe County is in the west of the state, a rather pretty and rural area that became a byword for claptrap.

In 1820 the Congress of the United States was debating the Missouri Question. The Missouri Question was to do with slavery and the answer turned out to be the Missouri Compromise. Towards the end of the debate a congressman called Felix Walker stood up, cleared his throat, began to speak and wouldn't stop.

He went on and on until people started to get fidgety, and on and on until people started to get annoyed, and on and on until people started to jeer, and on and on until people started to tap him on the shoulder and tell him to stop, and on and on until there was a small crowd round him demanding to know *why* he wouldn't stop.

Felix Walker replied that he was not speaking to Congress, his speech was for the benefit of his constituency back home: he was making "a speech for Buncombe."

You see, Felix Walker didn't care about the Missouri Question or the Missouri Compromise: he cared about the press coverage he would get among the voters in his own constituency. It was such an ingenious idea (and such a common practice in all democracies) that the phrase caught on, and *speaking to Buncombe* soon got shortened to *speaking bunkum* and then just plain *bunkum*, which needs to be *debunked*.

It's worthwhile mentioning that though that's the usual story, there's an alternative version in which a congressman wandered in and found Felix Walker addressing an utterly empty chamber. He asked Walker what the hell he was doing and Walker explained that he was speaking to Buncombe (no doubt a copy of the speech would be mailed home). I prefer this version, but it's less likely to be true. Either way, *bunkum* remains talk that serves no actual purpose, and is definitely down to the place in North Carolina.

Poor Buncombe County! Consigned to the dictionary as a byword for nonsense, Edward Buncombe must be turning in his grave.

Edward Buncombe was a British chap who was born in St. Kitt's but moved to America when he inherited a great big plantation in Carolina. He was one of the first fellows in the area to join the pro-independence movement, and when the Revolutionary War broke out in 1775 he joined the Continental Army and was wounded at the Battle of Germantown. He would probably have recovered were it not that one night he got out of bed and sleepwalked to the top of a flight of stairs, toppled down, and died from his re-opened wounds.

In his will he left over two thousand acres of plantation, and ten negroes. He was such a hero that a few years later Buncombe County was named in his honour. So really it's Edward Buncombe whose name is in *debunked*. Or you can go further.

Edward Buncombe must, somehow or other, have been a descendant of Richard de Bounecombe who lived in Somerset in the early fourteenth century. Bounecombe itself means *reedy (boune) valley (combe)*. *Combe* is one of the very few words in Old English that comes from Celtic. Why there are so few is a great mystery, and it all depends on how nasty the Anglo-Saxons were.

The Anglo-Saxon Mystery

Once upon a time, two thousand years ago, the British Isles were inhabited by Celts, who, as you might expect, spoke Celtic languages. They also had tattoos. The ancient Greeks called the inhabitants of these foggy islands *Prittanoi* (from where we get the name Britain), meaning *tattooed people*, although this may just have been down to the Celtic habit of painting themselves with woad, which the Greeks thought rather odd.

The important thing for the moment is that Boadicea (died 61 A.D.) wasn't *English*, even though she lived in what is now England. England didn't exist at the time. Boadicea was a Celtic Briton.

England started to exist only when the Angles began arriving from Denmark in about 400 A.D. They referred to their new country as *Angle-land* or *England*. Along with the Angles came the Saxons (from Saxony) and the Jutes (from Jutland) and between them they started to speak Old English.

Soon they had kings and one of these was called Alfred the Great, who was originally the King of the West Saxons but decided to call himself *Rex Angul-Saxonum*, or *King of the Anglo-Saxons*.

So what happened to the Celts? What happened to all the people who had swanned around the island before, covered in woad?

The answer is that nobody's quite sure. There are two arguments: the linguistic one and the historical one.

Whenever one bunch of people conquers another, they pick up a bit of the conquered people's language. You can't help it. Try as you might, the native language is all around you. You may have enslaved the natives, but you still need to be able to order your slaves around. You may not want to learn the language, but there are always new things in a new country that you don't have any words of your own to describe.

Take the example of the British in India. The Brits were there only for a couple of hundred years and yet in that time they picked up *shampoo, bungalow, juggernaut, mongoose, khaki, chutney, bangle, cushy, pundit, bandana, dinghy* et cetera. And those were only the words that they brought home with them.

So what words did the Angles and Saxons pick up from the Celts?

Next to nothing.

There's *combe*, meaning *valley*, which comes from *cym*. There's *tor*, meaning *rock*, which comes from *torr*, the Celtic word for *hill*. There's *cross*, which we seem to have got from Irish missionaries in the tenth century, rather than from the native Celts. And there's . . .

Well, there's not much else. It depends on how you count things, really, and it's always possible that words were there but not noted down. The Anglo-Saxons managed to occupy an island for hundreds of years and take almost no words from the people they defeated.

In fact, linguistically, this doesn't look like an occupation, it looks like a massacre. On the surface it would appear to be a pretty crazy massacre as well. Of course, massacres are always pretty bad things, but you'd still expect a *few* more words to have crept into Old English, even if they were only the words for *ouch*, *no* and *stop it*. In English there's a terrifying absence.

And the historians say that this is absolute hogwash. Where, they ask quite reasonably, are the bodies? There aren't any. No mass graves, no accounts of epic battles. No slaughter recorded. Nothing archaeological. Zero. Zilch. Nil.

So where linguists see a slaughter, archaeologists see

peaceful co-existence. It's all rather odd. Although there's a third possibility, which is illustrated by a hill in Herefordshire called Pensax, and a town in Essex called Saffron Walden.

Pensax means *hill (pen) of the Saxons*, and very importantly the *pen* there is a Celtic word. So it would seem that, for a while at least, there were Saxons on the hill and Celts down in the valley. The same goes for the charmingly named Dorset village of Sixpenny Handley. *Sixpenny* is a corruption of *Sex Pen* and is just Pensax with the elements swapped around.

Meanwhile, Saffron Walden is obviously a place where they grew saffron, but the *Walden* is odd. It's an Anglo-Saxon term meaning, literally, *valley of the foreigners*, but *wealh* was a word that was always used to refer to Celts (and, indeed, it gave us the name *Wales*).

So, if you work from the place-name evidence you get a third and very odd picture of a country filled with settlements of Anglo-Saxons and Celts living side by side, but *never* talking. That would mean that they weren't trading, weren't marrying, weren't doing anything at all except naming each other's settlements, presumably as places to avoid.

You might theorise that each people understood the other's language and merely chose to speak their own pure dialect, but it would appear that this wasn't the case. Again it comes down to place-names.

As we have seen, *pen* was a Celtic word for *hill*. Yet when the Old English came across a hill called *Pen*, they decided to name it *Pen hul*, *hul* being the Old English word for *hill*.

The same process was repeated all across England. Names were doubled up, such as *Bredon* (*hill hill*) or the *River Esk* (*river river*). This would seem to point to a linguistic exchange that didn't go much further than finding out a place-name before driving out anybody who knew what the place-name meant.

It also makes for some very amusing etymologies. *Penhul* became *Pendle* and then a few hundred years later somebody again noticed that it was a hill and changed the name to *Pendle Hill*, which means *Hill-Hill Hill*. This was not a one-off. Bredon Hill in Worcestershire is also *Hill-Hill Hill* on exactly the same pattern of Celtic (*bre*), Old English (*don*) and modern English (*hill*).

We will never know how the Anglo-Saxons and the Celts really got on. Maybe it was a massacre, maybe it was a jolly party. The ages were too dark and history is too forget-ful. Nor is it wise to be consumed by sorrow or anger. If you look back far enough everything is stolen and every country invaded. The Celts themselves had conquered the previous people of Britain around 600 B.C., and the Anglo-Saxons were about to get hit by the vicious Vikings, who would bring with them their own language and their own place-names. For example, one Viking found a sedge-covered stream in Yorkshire and decided to name it *Sedge-Stream*, thus spawning one of the world's largest corporations.

The Sedge-Strewn Stream and Globalisation

The Vikings were horrid people to whom history has, for some strange reason, been very indulgent. Whether it was the rape, the killing or the human sacrifice that you objected to, it was probably a bad thing when the Vikings arrived at Lindisfarne in 793 and then began to work their way down the northeast coast of England. They quickly got to Yorkshire, and near what is now Harrogate one of them found a sedge-strewn stream and decided to name it *Sedge-Stream*. Except of course he didn't call it that because *Sedge-Stream* would be English; he called it *Sedge-Stream* in Old Norse, and the Old Norse for *Sedge-Stream* is *Starbeck*.

Starbeck is now a little suburb on the eastern edge of Harrogate. The stream is still there, although there's no discernible sedge and it runs quite a bit of its way underground in a pipe next to the railway tracks. The place-name is first recorded in 1817, but, as we've seen, it must go back to the Vikings, and we also know that there were people there in the fourteenth century.

These people had sex (as people almost invariably do) and produced a family. The family was named for the place where they lived, almost. One vowel was changed. The Starbuck family are first recorded living in just the right area in 1379. Since then two things have happened: the Quaker movement was founded and America was discovered.

The result of this double catastrophe was that among the

first settlers of Nantucket Island near Cape Cod was a Quaker family whose name was Starbuck. Exactly how much they quaked is not recorded, but they did become big players in Nantucket's biggest trade: whaling.

The Starbuck family took up their harpoons with a vengeance. They were soon the most famous whalers in Nantucket if not the world. In 1823 Valentine Starbuck was chartered by the King and Queen of Hawaii to take them on a trip to England, where the unfortunate royal pair died of measles. Obed Starbuck discovered Starbuck Island in the Pacific and named it in honour of his cousin.*

A little over twenty years later, a man called Herman Melville began to write a novel about whales and whaling. Specifically he wrote about a ship called the *Pequod* setting sail from Nantucket to hunt a white whale known as Moby-Dick. Melville had been a whaler himself and had heard of the famous Starbuck whalers of Nantucket, so he decided to call the first mate of the *Pequod* Starbuck in their honour.

Moby-Dick wasn't a very popular novel at first. Most people, especially the British, couldn't make head or tail of it, though this was largely because the British edition was missing the last chapter. However, in the twentieth century, novels that nobody can make head or tail of became very much the fashion and *Moby-Dick* was taken up by all and sundry, especially American schoolteachers who have been inflicting

---

*History is actually rather bewildered as to who named it in honour of whom first.

its purple prose on children ever since. There was one particular English teacher in Seattle who loved the book: his name was Jerry Baldwin.

Baldwin and two friends wanted to start a coffee shop. They needed a name and Jerry Baldwin knew exactly where to find the right one—in the pages of *Moby-Dick*. He told his business partners of his fantastic idea. They were going to call the coffee shop . . .

Wait for it . . .

Pequod!

His business partners pointed out (quite rightly) that if you're planning to open a shop selling potable fluids, you probably don't want the name to contain the syllable *pee*. That's just bad marketing. So Baldwin was overruled and the others started looking for something a little more local. On a map of the area they found an old mining settlement in the Rocky Mountains called Camp Starbo. Baldwin's two partners decided that Starbo was a great name. But Jerry Baldwin was not to be defeated. He suggested that they compromise with a little alteration to the second syllable that would make the name match the *Pequod*'s first mate: *Starbucks*. The three of them agreed, and that Viking's name for a little stream in Yorkshire became one of the most famous brands in the world.

The high street might be a different place if Baldwin had remembered that Moby-Dick was based on a real white whale that was said to have fought off over a hundred whaling parties in the Pacific of the early nineteenth century: that whale was called Mocha Dick.

There are no branches of Starbucks on Starbuck Island, but that's probably because there are no people there either, and the occasional seal is unlikely to have the cash for a cappuccino.

Coffee

Balzac once wrote that:

> This coffee falls into your stomach, and straightway there is a general commotion. Ideas begin to move like the battalions of the Grand Army of the battlefield, and the battle takes place. Things remembered arrive at full gallop, ensuing to the wind. The light cavalry of comparisons deliver a magnificent deploying charge, the artillery of logic hurry up with their train and ammunition, the shafts of wit start up like sharpshooters. Similes arise, the paper is covered with ink; for the struggle commences and is concluded with torrents of black water, just as a battle with powder.

But Shakespeare never drank coffee. Nor did Julius Caesar, or Socrates. Alexander the Great conquered half the world without even a café latte to perk him up in the morning. The pyramids were designed and constructed without a whiff of a sniff of caffeine. Coffee was introduced to Europe only in 1615.

The achievements of antiquity are quite enough to cow the modern human, but when you realise that they did it all without caffeine it becomes almost unbearable. The words for coffee arrange themselves beautifully into highly caffeinated spirals. Let's start with *espressos* and consider what they have to do with *expressing* yourself.

An espresso is made in a little machine that *presses* steam *outwards* (*e* in Italian) through tightly packed grains of coffee. It's exactly the same process by which a cow *expresses* milk, or a sore *expresses* pus, and metaphorically it's the same process by which your thoughts are *expressed* outwards from your brain through your mouth. Thus *self-expression*.

Those actions that have been thought about are premeditated, intentional and deliberate. If, for example, you have done something *expressly* for a purpose, it's because you have thought about it.

How does this connect to *express* mail? *Expressly* came to mean *for one particular purpose*. A letter can be entrusted either to the tender mercies of the national postal system (who will probably lose it, burn it or deliver it back to you a month later with a fine) or it can be given to a paid messenger who has one *express* job: to deliver that one letter. This is an *express* delivery—one where a postman has been hired *expressly* for the purpose.

And the same is true of trains. Some trains stop at every station; no village halt or stray cow is too small or too irrelevant to slow you down. All this can be avoided if rather than taking a stopping train you board one that is bound *expressly* for one particular destination. Such trains are now known as *express* trains, and they usually have a little buffet car where you can pay a small fortune for a tiny *espresso*.

Cappuccino Monks

If expressive espressos have a circuitous etymology, it's as nothing compared to the frothy delights of the *cappuccino*.

In 1520, a monk called Matteo Da Bascio decided that his fellow Franciscans were all terrible sybarites who had fallen away from the original calling of Saint Francis. They did luxurious things like wearing shoes, and Da Bascio decided to start a new order of pure, barefoot Franciscans.

The Old Franciscans were rather hurt by this and tried to suppress Matteo's unshod breakaways. He was forced to flee into hiding with the sympathetic Camaldolese monks who wore *little hoods* called, in Italian, *cappuccios*. Matteo and his brethren wore the cappuccios themselves, just to blend in, but when his breakaway order got official recognition in 1528, they found that they had become so used to the hoods that they decided to keep them on. His followers were therefore nicknamed the *Capuchin Monks*.

The Capuchin Monks spread quickly all over Catholic Europe, and their hoods had become so familiar that when, a century later, explorers in the New World found apes with a dark brown patch on the top of their heads that looked like a little monkey-hood, they decided to call them *Capuchin Monkeys*.

What's particularly beautiful about this name is that, so far as anybody can tell, *monkeys* are named after *monks*. You see, most people agreed with Matteo Da Bascio: far from being models of chastity and virtue, medieval monks were all filthy sinners and little better than animals. So what do you call that brown, hairy ape? A *mon*key.

The habit of the Capuchin Order was, and is, a pretty sort of creamy brown colour. So when the new, frothy, creamy, chocolate-sprinkled form of coffee was invented in the first half of the twentieth century, it was named after their robes: the *cappuccino*.

Mind you, most baristas wouldn't understand you if you ordered a *little hood*. But then again, most *baristas* don't realise that they are really *barristers*.

Called to the Bar

Barista, the chap who serves you your coffee, is a case of English lending a word to Italian and then taking it straight back again. A *barista* is nothing more than an Italian *barman*. The *–ist* suffix just means *practitioner*, as in a Marx*ist* evangel*ist*.

A *bar*, as any good dictionary will tell you, is *a rod of wood or iron that can be used to fasten a gate*. From this came the idea of a *bar* as any let or hindrance that can stop you going where you want to; specifically the *bar* in a pub or tavern is the *bar*-rier behind which is stored all the lovely intoxicating liquors that only the *bar*man is allowed to lay his hands on without forking out.

We are all, at times, called to the bar, if only in order to pay the bill. But the bar to which *barristers* were called was a lot less alcoholic, even though it was in an inn.

Half a millennium ago, all English lawyers were required to train at the Inns of Court in London. These inns were not the pleasant inns that serve beer, they were merely lodging houses for students of the law, because *inn*, originally, just meant *house*.

The internal arrangement of the Inns of Court was as Byzantine and incomprehensible as one would expect from a building devoted to the law, but basically there were the *Readers*, who were clever folk and sat in an Inner Sanctum separated from the rest of the students by a big *bar*.

The lesser students would sit around reading and study-ing and dreaming of the great day when they would be *called to the bar* and allowed to plead a case like a proper lawyer. The situation was complicated by the fact that there used to be *outer barristers* and *inner barristers* who had a particular relationship with sheriffs at law, and you would probably have to study for a few years before you understood the bar system even partially, and it wouldn't do you any good any-way, as just when you thought you'd got a grip on things, the meaning of *bar* was changed. That's law for you.

In about 1600 the word *bar* started to be applied to a wooden railing that ran around every courtroom in England, at which prisoners had to stand while the judge ticked them off or sentenced them or fumbled with his black cap. The defendant's *barr*ister would stand next to him at the bar and plead his case.

Meanwhile, the prosecuting lawyer would insist that the prisoner was guilty and that he was ready to prove his case. If he insisted this in French he would say *Culpable: prest d'averrer nostre bille*, but that was a bit of a mouthful so it would be shortened to *cul-prit*.

Then the defendant's fate would be handed over to a jury. If the jury couldn't decide, then they would declare *we don't know*, but they would declare it in Latin—and the Latin for *we don't know* is *ignoramus*.

Ignoramus was thus a technical legal term until a writer called George Ruggle used it as the title for a play in 1615, the main character of which was a stupid lawyer called *Ignoramus*. The usage stuck and now an ignoramus is any old idiot.

This also means that the plural of *ignoramus* is definitely not *ignorami*.

Ignorami

Christians are all cretins, etymologically speaking, and cretins are all Christians. If this sounds unfair, it's because language is much less kind than religion.

The original cretins were deformed and mentally deficient dwarves found only in a few remote valleys in the Alps. These days their condition would be called *congenital iodine deficiency syndrome*, but the Swiss didn't know anything about that. All they knew was that, though these people had a problem, they were still human beings and fellow Christians. So they called them *Cretins*, which means *Christians*.

They meant this in a nice way. It was like calling them *fellow humans*, but of course the word got taken up by bullies and, like *spastic* in modern playgrounds, *cretin* quickly acquired a derogatory sense. So *Christian* became a term of abuse.

The first *idiots* were also Christian, or rather the first Christians were *idiots*. The word *idiot* first appears in English in the Wycliffite Bible of 1382. There, in the Book of Deeds (which we would call Acts), it says that:

Forsoth thei seynge the stedfastnesse of Petre and John, founden that thei weren men with oute lettris, and idiotis

A verse that was translated in the King James Version as:

Now when they saw the boldness of Peter and John, and perceived that they were unlearned and ignorant men

But in the Latin of Saint Jerome, the passage ran:

> *videntes autem Petri constantiam et Iohannis conperto quod*
> *homines essent sine litteris et idiotae*

Saint Peter and Saint John were *idiots* simply because they were *laymen*. They had no qualifications and were therefore their own men, rather than belonging to some professional class. If they had spoken *their own* language it would have been an *idiom*, and if they had been eccentrics with their *own way of doing things* (which they undoubtedly were) they would have been *idiosyncratic*.

Neither *cretin* nor *idiot* was originally meant to be an insult. One was a compliment and the other a simple description, but people are cruel and are always casting about for new ways to abuse others. As fast as we can think up technical terms and euphemisms like *cretin, moron, idiot* or *spastic*, people will take the words and use them to be nasty to others. Consider the poor *moron*. The term was invented in 1910 by the American Association for the Study of the Feeble-Minded. They took an obscure Greek word, *moros*, which meant *dull* or *foolish*, and used it to refer to those with an IQ of between 50 and 70. The idea was that it would be a word reserved for doctors and diagnosis. Within seven years the word had escaped from medical circles and was being used as an insult.

Incidentally, *moron* meant *dull*, but in Greek *oxy* meant *sharp*. Many, many chapters ago we saw how *oxygen* got its name because it *gen*erated acids, and the *oxy* in *oxymoron* has the same root. So an *oxymoron* is a *sharp softness*.

The unkindest twist of the English language is, perhaps,

that which happened to John Duns Scotus (1265–1308). He was the greatest theologian and thinker of his day, the *Doctor Subtilis*, the philosopher of the univocity of being, master of the formal distinction and of the concept of haecceity, the essential property that makes each thing this, and not that.

Duns Scotus had a formidable mind, which he used to draw the finest distinctions between different ideas. This was, linguistically, his downfall and destruction.

When Duns Scotus died his many followers and disciples lived on. They pursued and expanded on his astonishingly complicated philosophical system of distinctions and differences. One could almost say that they, like their master, were hair-splitters and pedants.

In fact, people did say they were hair-splitters and pedants. When the Renaissance came along, people suddenly got rather enlightened and humanist and were terribly angry when *Duns-men*, as they were called, tried to contradict them with an obscure Aristotelian enthymeme. Duns-men became the enemies of progress, the idiots who would turn the clock back and return to the Dark Ages; and *Duns* started to be spelled *dunce*.

Thus did the greatest mind of his generation become a synonym for *gormless*. This is terribly unfair, as Duns Scotus was full of *gorm*. He was brimming over with the stuff. And if you don't know what *gorm* is, that's because it's a fossil word.

Fossil-less

Do you have any gorm? It's an important question, because if you don't have any gorm it logically follows that you are gormless. *Gormless* is a fossil. Dinosaurs and trilobites once flourished, now only fossils remain, petrified and scattered. The same has happened to *gorm*, *feck*, *ruth* and *reck*. They were all once real words. Now they are frozen forever in *–less* phrases.

Gorm (spelled all sorts of ways) was a Scandinavian word meaning *sense* or *understanding*. As a twelfth-century monk called Orm put it:

& yunnc birrþ nimenn mikell gom
To þæwenn yunnkerr chilldre

—a sentiment with which we can all, I'm sure, agree. However, poor *gorm* (or *gome*) rarely got written down. It was a dialect word used by Yorkshiremen, and most of the literary action was happening in London.

However, in the nineteenth century Emily Brontë wrote a book called *Wuthering Heights*, in which is the line:

Did I ever look so stupid: so gormless as Joseph calls it?

Joseph is a servant who speaks with a strong Yorkshire accent, and the word *gormless* is clearly being brought in as an example of one of his dialect terms. Joseph would probably have used the word *gorm* as well, but Emily Brontë doesn't mention it. So *gormless* got into one of the most famous novels ever written, while poor *gorm* was left to pine away and die on a lonely moor in Yorkshire.

Once upon a time there was the word *effect*. It was a happy, useful, innocent word until it went to Scotland. Once north of Hadrian's Wall, the word *effect* was cruelly robbed of its extremities and became *feck*.

Indolent, vigourless Scotsmen who had no ef*fect* on things were therefore *feckless*. This time it was not Brontë but Thomas Carlyle, a Scot, who brought the word into common usage. He used *feckless* to describe the Irish and his wife.

However, it's hard to see exactly what Carlyle meant by *feckless*. This is from a letter of 1842:

> Poor Allan's dust was laid in Kensal Green,—far enough from his native Kirkmahoe. M'Diarmid has a well-meant but very feckless Article upon him this week.

In another letter Carlyle wrote that the summer had made his wife feckless, and he even described how living with her in London had turned the couple into "a feckless pair of bodies," "a pair of miserable creatures." Anyway, Carlyle used *feckless* but he never used the word *feck*, and so the one word lived and became famous, while the other vanished into a Celtic twilight.

Reckless is far simpler and there's more poetry in it, which is the important thing. *Reck* used to mean *care* (although it's etymologically far from *reckon*). As Chaucer put it:

> I recke nought what wrong that thou me proffer,
> For I can suffer it as a philosopher.

Shakespeare used *reck* too, yet by his time it already had an archaic feel. In *Hamlet*, Ophelia chides her brother thus:

> Do not as some ungracious pastors do,
> Show me the steep and thorny way to heaven,
> Whiles, like a puff'd and reckless libertine,
> Himself the primrose path of dalliance treads
> And recks not his own rede.

Rede was an archaic and ancient word for *advice*, and *reck* was probably already an archaic and ancient word for *take notice of*. Shakespeare used *reckless* six times in his complete works, as much as all the other *recks*, *recketbs* and *reckeds* put together. *Reck* must already have been fading, *reckless* rushing headlong to the future.

If something is *true*, it's the *truth*. If you *rue* your actions, you feel *ruth*. If you don't rue your actions, you feel no ruth and that makes you *ruthless*. *Ruth* survived for quite a long time, and it's uncertain as to why it died out in the end. Maybe it's just that there are more ruthless people than ruthful ones.

Language sometimes doesn't have an explanation. Words rise and die for no reason that an etymologist can discover.

History is not immaculate; in fact, it is *maculate*. We might feel more *consolate* if we could give a span, and even spick, explanation for everything, but to no avail.

And so we come, *exorably*, to the end of our study of fossil words. We could go on, as the language is brimming with them, but you might become listless and disgruntled. P. G. Wodehouse once remarked of a chap that, "if not exactly disgruntled he was far from being gruntled." So let us continue by seeing exactly how *gruntling* relates to *grunt*.

The Frequentative Suffix

If a gem frequently sparks, we say that it *sparkles*. If a burning log frequently emits cracking noises, then it *crackles*. That's because *–le* is a frequentative suffix.

With this in mind, let's turn to *grunting*. To *gruntle* is to *grunt often*. If a pig makes one noise it has grunted, if it grunts again you may add the frequentative suffix and call the pig a *gruntler*. A medieval travel writer called Sir John Mandeville*

---

*There never was a Sir John Mandeville, but there is a book by him. That's how authorship worked in the fourteenth century. Moreover, I have modernised the quotation to make it comprehensible. The *gruntle* is spelt *gruntils* in the original.

described the men who live in the desert near the Garden of Eden thus:

> In that desert are many wild men, that are hideous to look on; for they are horned, and they speak not, but gruntle, as swines do.

But the *dis* in *disgruntled* is not a negative prefix but an intensive one. If the verb already carries negative connotations (and something that makes you keep grunting is probably no good), then the negative *dis* just emphasises how bad it is. *Disgruntled* therefore means almost the same thing as *gruntled*.

Some frequentatives are a little more surprising. The next time you are being *jostled* in a crowd, you may reflect that your fate is rather milder than somebody who is repeatedly being attacked by a *jousting* knight. Medieval lovers used to *fond* each other, and if they did this too often, they began to *fondle*. Fondling is a dangerous business, as sooner or later it leads to *snugging*, an archaic word that meant *to lie down together in order to keep warm*. Repeated incidences of *snugging* will result in *snuggling*, and pregnancy.

Whether you *trample*, *tootle*, *wrestle* or *fizzle*, you are being frequentative. So here's a little puzzle (a *puzzle* being a question that is frequently *posed*). What are the originals of these frequentatives?

Nuzzle
Bustle
Waddle

Straddle
Swaddle*

Of course, the reason that you can't get all those immediately is that a frequentative often leaves home and starts to be a word in its own right. Take the Latin *pensare*, which meant *to think* and from which we get the words *pensive* and *pansy* (a flower given to a loved one to make them think of you). The Romans thought that thinking was nothing more than *repeatedly weighing things up*. So *pensare* is a frequentative of *pendere*, *to weigh or hang*, from which we get more words than you might think.

Pending

The Latin *pendere* meant *to hang*, and its past participle was *pensum. In* meant *not*, *de* meant *from*, *sus* meant *down* . . .

If you are inde*pendent* you are not de*pendent* because the only things that are de*pendent* are *pend*ulums and *pend*ants that *hang* around your neck. *Pend*ants are therefore *pend*ing, or indeed im*pend*ing. They are, at least, sus*pended*, and are therefore left hanging in sus*pense*.

---

*And the answers are: *nose*, *burst*, *wade*, *stride* and *swathe*.

Weighing scales *hang* in the balance. Scales can weigh out gold for paying *pens*ions, sti*pend*s and com*pens*ations in *pes*os (but not *pence*, which is etymologically unrelated).

All such dis*pens*ations must, of course, be weighed up mentally. One must be *pens*ive before being ex*pens*ive. You must give equal weight to all arguments in order to have either equi*poise* or *poise*. If you don't give equal weight to all things, your scales will hang too much to one side and you will end up with a pre*pond*erance and pro*pens*ity towards your own *pen*chants. Whether these *pen*chants make you per*pend*icular, I am too polite to ask.

I hope that this section on the *pend*ulous hung together. If it did, it was a com*pend*ium. And though there are a few more words from the same root, to include them all would require the ap*pend*ing of an ap*pend*ix.

An appendix, in either a book or a body, is where you put all the useless crap. However, the bodily tube is more properly known as the *vermiform appendix*, which makes it sound even less pleasant than it is, because *vermiform* means *wormlike*, which is something to consider next time you eat *vermicelli*.

Worms and their Turnings

Worms have a hard time. When not being chased about by early birds or being disturbed in their can, they get trodden on. It's no surprise that Shakespeare records them fighting back against their oppressors:

> The smallest worm will turn, being trodden on,
> And doves will peck in safeguard of their brood.

William Blake, on the other hand, claimed that "The cut worm forgives the plow," which seems extraordinarily unlikely.

Etymologically, it's hardly surprising that worms turn. *Worm* comes from the Proto-Indo-European *wer*, meaning *turn*, a reference to their bendiness. So a *worm turning* is not just appropriate, it's a tautology.

Worms have come a long way down in the world, as the word *worm* used to mean *dragon*. Then from a huge fire-breathing monster they became mere *snakes*, and slowly they declined until they became the little things in your garden being chased around by a blackbird (or sliced up by William Blake). However, the *dragon* meaning survived for centuries, and as late as 1867 William Morris could still write the wonderful line, "Therewith began a fearful battle twixt worm and man," with a straight face.

The one constant in the etymological journey of the worm is that man doesn't like worms and worms don't like men. For a long time it was believed that garden worms could crawl into your ear, and as the Old English *wicga* could also mean worm, we get the strange modern formation *earwig*, even though an earwig is technically not a worm but an insect and has nothing to do with the sort of wig you wear on your head.*

There are only two places where worms have turned and maintained some of their former greatness. One is a *worm-hole*, which used to mean exactly what you might expect until 1957 when the word was hijacked by the Einstein-Rosen Bridge, a theoretical connection between two parts of space-time implied, if not necessitated, by the Theory of Relativity.

The other is the fearsome crocodile, whose name comes from the Greek *kroke-drilos*, which means *pebble-worm*. Pebbles also play a crucial part in *calculus*, which means *pebble*.

Mathematics

Mathematics is an abstract discipline of such austere beauty that it's often surprising to find that its words and symbols have dull, concrete origins. *Calculus* is a formidable word

---

*Although people do wear wigs in odd places. Seventeenth-century prostitutes used to shave their economic areas in order to get rid of lice, and then wear a special pubic wig called a *merkin*. And while we're on the subject of earwigs, ear hair grows from a place medically known as the *tragus* because *tragos* was Greek for goat, and ear hair resembles a goat's beard. Ancient Athenian actors used to wear goat-skin when they acted in serious plays, which is why the plays came to be known as *the songs of the goat*, or *tragedies*.

that loses some of its grandeur when you realise that a *calculus* is just a little pebble, because the Romans did their maths by counting up stones.

Oddly, an abacus, which you might reasonably have expected to mean *little pebbles*, comes ultimately from the Hebrew word *abaq* meaning *dust*. You see, the Greeks, who adopted the word, didn't use pebbles; instead they used a board covered with sand, on which they could write out their calculations. When they wanted to start on a new sum, they simply shook the board and it became clear, like a classical Etch A Sketch.

Average has an even more mundane explanation. It comes from the Old French *avarie*, which meant *damage done to a ship*. Ships were often co-owned and when one was damaged and the bill came in for repairs, each owner was expected to pay the *average*.

A *line* is only a thread from a piece of *linen*, a *trapezium* is only a *table*, and a *circle* is only a *circus*. But the best of the mathematical etymologies are in the signs.

People didn't used to write 1 + 1, they would write the sentence *I et I*, which is Latin for *one and one*. To make the plus sign, all they did was drop the *e* in *et* and leave the crossed +. By coincidence, *ET* also gave us &, and you can see how & became & simply by messing around with the typefaces on your word processor. Type an & and then switch the font to Trebuchet and you'll get &, to French Script MT and you'll get &, to Curlz MT and you'll get &, Palatino Linotype and you'll get & and finally, as this book is printed in Adobe Caslon, you get &.

Most mathematics used to be written out in full sentences, which is why the equals sign was invented by a sixteenth-century Welshman who rejoiced in the name of Robert Recorde. Robert had got thoroughly bored of writing out the words *is equal to* every time he did a sum. This was particularly irritating for him, as he was writing a mathematical textbook with the memorable title, *The Whetestone of Witte whiche is the seconde parte of Arithmeteke: containing the extraction of rootes; the cossike practise, with the rule of equation; and the workes of Surde Nombers.*

But the prolixity of the title was matched by the brevity that the book brought to algebra. Recorde wrote:

> . . . to avoid the tedious repetition of these words: is equal to: I will set as I do often in work use, a pair of parallels, or Gemowe lines of one length, thus: =, bicause no 2 things, can be more equal.

So = is an equals sign because the two lines are of *equal* length. Robert Recorde published his *Whetstone of* . . . (see above) in 1557 and died in debtors' prison the following year, thus demonstrating the difference between good mathematics and good accounting.

Recorde thought that the two lines of = were so similar that they were like identical twins, which is why he called them *gemowe*, meaning *twin*. *Gemowe* derived from the Old French *gemeaus*, which was the plural of *gemel*, which came from the Latin *gemellus*, which was the diminutive of *Gemini*.

Stellafied and Oily Beavers

The zodiac is, of course, the little circular *zoo* that runs around the sky. It's a *zoo*-diac because eleven of the twelve signs are living creatures and seven of them are animals. In fact, when the Greeks named the zodiac all of the signs were living creatures. *Libra*, the odd one out, was added in by the Romans.

The zodiac is filled with all sorts of strange word associations. *Cancer* is the *crab* largely because Galen thought that some tumours resembled crabs and partly because both words come from the Indo-European root *qarq*, which meant *hard*. Goats such as *Capricorn* skip about and are generally *capricious*, or *goatlike*. And bulls like *Taurus* get killed by *toreadors*. But let's stick, for the moment, to *Gemini*, the *twins*.

The twins in question are two stars called Castor and Pollux, and how they came to be there is a tender and touching story. Despite what astronomers would have you believe, most of the stars were created not by energy cooling into matter, but by Zeus.

Zeus had a thing for a girl called Leda and decided to turn into a swan and have his wicked way with her. However, later that night Leda slept with her husband Tyndareus. The result was a rather complicated pregnancy and Leda popping out two eggs, which is enough to make any husband suspicious.

The first egg contained Helen (of Troy) and Clytemnestra. The second egg contained Pollux and Castor. Extensive mythological paternity testing revealed that Helen and Pollux were the children of Zeus, and Castor and Clytemnestra were the mortal children of Tyndareus, which can hardly have been much of a consolation for the poor chap.

Castor and Pollux were inseparable until one day Castor was stabbed and killed. Pollux, who was a demi-god, struck a deal with his dad that he could share his immortality with his twin brother, and the result was that Zeus turned them into two stars that could be together forever in the heavens (well, in fact, they're sixteen light years apart, but let's not get bogged down in details).

Castor was the Greek word for *beaver*, and to this day beavers all across the world belong to the genus *Castor*, even if they don't know it. We usually think of beavers as sweet little creatures who build dams, but that's not how a constipated Renaissance man would view them; a constipated Renaissance man would view them as his relief and his cure.

You see, the beaver has two sacs in his groin that contain a noxious and utterly disgusting oil that acts as a very effective laxative. This very valuable liquid was known as *castor oil*.

The name survives, but the source of the liquid has changed. To the delight of beavers everywhere, people discovered in the mid-eighteenth century that you can get exactly the same bowel-liberating effect from an oil produced from the seeds of *Ricinus communis*, also known as the castor oil plant. So though it's still called castor oil, it's no longer obtained from the groin of a beaver.

Several anatomical terms derive from the beaver, but in order to keep this chain of thought decent and pure and family-friendly, let us for the moment consider that *beaver* was once a word for *beard*.

Beards

The number of hidden beards in the English language is quite bizarre. *Bizarre*, for example, comes from the Basque word *bizar* or *beard*, because when Spanish soldiers arrived in the remote and clean-shaven villages of the Pyrenees, the locals thought that their *bizars* were *bizarre*.

The feathers that were stuck into the back of arrows were known by the Romans as *the beard*, or *barbus*, which is why arrows are *barbs*, and that's ultimately the reason that *barbed* wire is simply wire that has grown a beard.

Barbus is also the reason that the man who cuts your beard is known as a *barber*. The ancient Romans liked to be clean-shaven, as beards were considered weird and Greek, so their barbers plied a regular and lucrative trade until the fall of the Roman empire. Italy was overrun by tribesmen who had huge long beards which they never even trimmed. These tribesmen were known as the *longa barba*, or *longbeards*, which was eventually shortened to *Lombard*, which is why a large part of northern Italy is still known as Lombardy.

The Romans by that time had become effete, perhaps through a lack of facial hair, and couldn't take their opponents on. If they had been more courageous and less shaven, they could have stood *beard to beard* against their enemies, which would have made them objectionable and *rebarbative*.

What the Romans needed was a leader like General Ambrose Burnside, who fought for the Union during the American Civil War. General Burnside had vast forests of hair running from his ears and connecting to his leviathan moustache. So extraordinary was his facial foliage that such growths came to be known as *burnsides*. However, Ambrose Burnside died and was forgotten, and later generations of Americans, reasoning that the hair was on the *side* of the face, took the name *burnside* and bizarrely swapped it around to make *sideburns*.

And it's not only humans that have beards, nor only animals. Even trees may forget to shave, namely the *giant bearded fig* of the Caribbean. The bearded fig is also known as the *strangler tree* and can grow to fifty feet in height. The beards and the height and the strangling are connected, for the tree reproduces by growing higher than its neighbours and then dropping beard-like aerial roots into their unsuspecting branches. The beards wrap themselves around the victim until they reach the ground, where they burrow in and then tighten, strangling the host.

There's an island in the Caribbean that's filled with them. The natives used to call it the *Red Land with White Teeth*, but the Spanish explorers who discovered it were so impressed with the psychotic and unshaven fig trees that they called it *The Bearded Ones*, or *Barbados*.

Islands

Some parts of the English language can only be reached by boat. For instance, there's a small dot in the middle of the Pacific Ocean whose natives called their home Coconut Island, or *Pikini*, which was mangled into English as *Bikini Atoll*.

For centuries nobody knew about Bikini except its natives, and even when it was discovered by Europeans, the best use that anyone could think of for the place was as a nautical graveyard. When a warship had outlived its effectiveness, it would be taken to the beautiful lagoon and sunk.

Bikini Atoll was put on the map (and almost removed from it) by America in 1946 when they tested their new atomic bombs there. *Atom* is Greek for *unsplittable*, but the Americans had discovered that by breaking the laws of etymology they were able to create vast explosions, and vast explosions were the best way of impressing the Soviets and winning the Cold War.

However, the tests at Bikini had a more immediate effect on the French and the Japanese—both, perhaps, illustrative of their national characters.

In 1954 the Americans tested their new hydrogen bomb, which they had calculated would be a little more powerful than the A-bombs they'd previously been mucking around with. It turned out to be an awful lot more powerful and ended up accidentally irradiating the crew of a Japanese fishing boat. Japanese public opinion was outraged, as the Japanese and

Americans had a rather awkward military and nuclear relationship. Protests were made, hackles were raised, and a film was made about an irresponsible nuclear test that awoke a sea monster called *Gorilla-whale* or *Gojira*. The film was rushed through production and came out later in the same year. *Gojira* was, allegedly, simply the nickname of a particularly burly member of the film crew. *Gojira* was anglicised to *Godzilla*, and the film became so famous across the world that –*zilla* became a workable English suffix.

A bride-to-be who has become obsessed with every fatuous detail of her nuptials from veil to hem is now called a bride*zilla*, and one of the world's most popular internet browsers is Mo*zilla* Firefox, whose name and old logo can be traced straight back to the tests at Bikini Atoll.

But where the Japanese saw a threatening monster, the French saw what the French always see: sex. A fashion designer called Jacques Heim had just come up with a design for a two-piece bathing costume that he believed would be the world's smallest swimsuit. He took it to a lingerie shop in Paris where the owner, Louis Réard, proved with a pair of scissors that it could be even more scandalously immodest. The result, Réard claimed, would cause an explosion of lust in the loins of every Frenchman so powerful that it could only be compared to the tests at Bikini Atoll, so he called the new swimwear the *bikini*.

So by a beautiful serendipity, it's now possible to log on to the internet and use a Mozilla browser to look at pictures of girls in bikinis, knowing that the two words spring from the same event.

The word *serendipity* was invented in 1754 by Horace Walpole, the son of the first prime minister of England. He was kind enough to explain exactly how he had come up with the word. He was reading a book called the *Voyage des trois princes de Serendip*, which is a story of three princes from the island of Serendip who are sent by their father to find a magical recipe for killing dragons. Walpole noticed that "as their highnesses travelled they were always making discoveries, by accidents and sagacity, of things which they were not in quest of." Though the story of the three princes that Walpole read was pure fiction, the Island of Serendip was a real place, although it has since changed its name, first to Ceylon, and then, in 1972, to Sri Lanka. So a *serendipity* is really a *Sri-Lanka-ness*.

Now let us cross the Indian Ocean and head up the Suez canal to Sardinia. In fact, let's not, because the people of Sardinia are a nasty bunch. In ancient times they were considered so waspish and rebarbative that any unfriendly remark would be referred to as *Sardinian*, which is where we get the word *sardonic*. However, Sardinia also gave its name to the little fish that were abundant in the surrounding seas, which are now called *sardines*.

We *could* go to the island of Lesbos, but that wouldn't make us very popular. The most famous resident of Lesbos was an ancient Greek poetess called Sappho. Sappho wrote ancient Greek poems about how much she liked other ancient Greek ladies, and the result was that in the late nineteenth century *Lesbian* became an English euphemism for ladies who like ladies. The idea, of course, was that only people with a good classical education would understand the reference, and people with a good classical education would have strong enough minds not to snigger. In this, *lesbianism* was considered preferable to the previous English term, *tribadism*, which came from a Greek word for *rubbing*.

Before being adopted in the 1890s, *Lesbian* was the name of a kind of wine that came from the island, so you could drink a good Lesbian. Of course, it also was, and is, the name for the inhabitants of the island, not all of whom are happy with the word's new meaning. In 2008 a group of Lesbians (from the island) tried to take out an injunction against a group of lesbians (from the mainland) to make them change the name of their gay rights association. The injunction failed, but just to be on the safe side, let us sail our etymological ship out through the straits for Gibraltar and head for the islands where dogs grow feathers.

The Romans found some islands in the Atlantic that were overrun with large dogs. So they called them the *Dog Islands* or *Canaria*. However, when the English finally got round to inspecting the Canaria a couple of millennia later, all they found there were birds, which they decided to call *canaries*, thus changing dogs into birds (and then into a pretty shade of yellow). Now let's continue due west to get to the Cannibal Islands.

When Christopher Columbus sailed west across the Atlantic, he arrived at the Caribbean Islands, which he rather hopefully called the *West Indies* because the purpose of his voyage had been to find a western route to *India*, which everyone in Europe knew to be a rich country ruled by the Great Khan.

Columbus was therefore terribly pleased when he landed in Cuba and discovered that the people there called themselves *Canibs*, because he assumed that *Can*ibs must really be *Khan*ibs, which was a rare triumph of hope over etymology. At the next island Columbus came to, they told him they were *Caribs*, and at the island after that they were *Calibs*. This was because in the old languages of the Caribbean, Ns, Rs and Ls were pretty much interchangeable.

The sea got named the *Carib*bean after one pronunciation. But it was also believed in Europe that the islanders ate each other, and this gastronomic perversity came, on the basis of another pronunciation, to be called *cannib*alism. Whether they did actually eat each other is a subject that is still disputed. Some say they did, others say that it was just a projection of European fears—and it's true that the European imagination was set humming by these stories of far-off islands. William Shakespeare's play *The Tempest* was set on a desert island where a strange half-man half-fish is the only true native. There definitely aren't any men-fish in the Caribbean, but that didn't stop Shakespeare from naming his bestial character *Calib*an after the third possible pronunciation.

But now we sail onwards through the Panama canal* to

---

*The neatest palindrome in English is undoubtedly: "A man, a plan, a canal: Panama."

the last of our island chain, Hawaii, after which the world's most popular snack was almost named.

Sandwich Islands

The first European to stand on the shores of Hawaii was Captain James Cook, who arrived there in 1778 and died there in 1779 after an unsuccessful attempt to abduct the king. Captain Cook introduced the words *tattoo* and *taboo* into English, both having been practices that he came across in his Pacific voyages, but there was one name that he couldn't get into the dictionary, or even the atlas.

European explorers loved to name the places that they discovered, a habit that didn't always endear them to the natives, who felt that they must have discovered the place first as they were already living there. So, although Cook noted down that the locals called his new discovery *Owyhee*, he knew which side his bread was buttered and decided to rename the place in honour of the sponsor of his voyage. Captain Cook was, of course, thinking of his future career (something that he should probably have considered when abducting the king), for Cook's sponsor was, at the time, the first lord of the admiralty: John Montagu, Fourth Earl of Sandwich.

But the name *Sandwich* didn't stick, and Cook died before his sponsor could even hear of the attempt. The poor

Earl of Sandwich has had to make do with the South Sandwich Islands (an uninhabited chain of rocks near the South Pole), Montague Island (an uninhabited island near Alaska), and every *sandwich* shop, *sandwich*-maker, and *sandwich* filling in the entire world. And he managed that latter feat without ever going near a bread knife.

The Earl of Sandwich was a gambler, and not just any sort of gambler. He was an addict who lost money hand over fist over hand over fist. Even by the British standards of the time he was considered a bit odd, and the British were famous for gambling. The first and only account of the origin of the world's favourite snack comes from a French book of 1765 about what terrible gamblers the English are. It runs thus:

> The English, who are profound thinkers, violent in their desires, and who carry all their passions to excess, are altogether extravagant in the art of gaming: several rich noblemen are said to have ruined themselves by it: others devote their whole time to it, at the expense of their repose and health. A minister of state passed four and twenty hours at a public gaming table, so absorbed in play, that, during the whole time, he had no subsistence but a bit of beef, between two slices of toasted bread, which he eat without ever quitting the game. The new dish grew highly in vogue, during my residence in London: it was called by the name of the minister who invented it.

The author didn't mention the name of the minister, because he was a Frenchman writing for a French audience in French;* so there would be no point in his explaining the origin of an English word. It's therefore a delicious twist in the tale that *sandwich* is now one of the few English words that everybody in France knows too.

There's a myth that the Earl of Sandwich *invented* the sandwich. He did not. He had servants and chefs to actually make his food for him. Sandwich simply made sandwiches cool. People have almost certainly been stuffing things between two slices of bread since the stuff was invented around the end of the last ice age. What the Earl of Sandwich did was to take a humble little snack that you wouldn't think twice about, and give it associations of aristocracy, power, wealth, luxury and twenty-four-hour gambling.

Great men and women do not busy themselves in the kitchen hoping to achieve the immortality that can be conferred by a recipe book. They simply wait until a food is named after them. Take Margherita Maria Teresa Giovanna, Queen of Italy and wife of Umberto I. She never climbed Mount Stanley, but Mount Stanley's highest peak still bears her name. She certainly never cooked any pizzas: they were made for her, and they had to be fit for a queen.

---

*In case you were wondering, the quotation reproduced here comes from a 1772 translation. From the fact that it doesn't even feel the need to mention sandwiches, we can assume that everybody in England now knew the name.

Italian aristocrats of the nineteenth century didn't eat pizza. It was peasant food, flavoured with that peasant favourite: garlic. However, in the 1880s, European royalty, wary of revolution, were all trying to be nice to the common men whom they ruled. So when King Umberto and Queen Margherita visited Naples, the home of the pizza, a man named Raffaele Esposito decided to make a pizza fit for the lips of the queen.

Esposito was the owner of the Pizzeria di Pietro e Basta Così, and he got over the garlic problem by simply not using any garlic, an idea that was previously unheard of. He then decided to make the pizza properly patriotic and Italian by modelling it on the colours of the flag: red, white and green. So he added tomatoes for the red (nobody had done this before), mozzarella for the white, and herbs for the green. He then named it *Pizza Margherita* and sent it, in June 1889, to the queen.

To be honest, Queen Margherita probably didn't deign to eat the first margherita, but she did have one of her servants write a note saying thank you. Thus has her name become immortal, and a coded version of the Italian flag is on the menu of every pizza restaurant in the world.

The Italian flag consists of three vertical stripes. This design is based on *le Tricolore*, the flag of the French Revolution.

The French Revolution in English Words

When the world changes, language changes. New things need new words, and the new words of a period betray the inventions of the age. The Vietnam War gave American English *bong* and *credibility gap*.

You can follow the history of the English-speaking world by watching the new words flow by. The forties gave us *genocide, quisling, crash-landing, debrief* and *cold war*. The fifties gave us *countdown, cosmonaut, sputnik* and *beatnik*. The sixties gave us *fast food, jetlag* and *fab*. And so on through *Watergate, yuppie, Britpop* and *pwned*.

But nothing has ever been as new as the French Revolution, which was essentially a mob of new ideas armed with pitchforks and intent on murder. Every new event, every new idea, had to be rendered for the English-speaking world in new words that were being imported from the French. Each twist, turn, beheading and storming was reported a few days later in Britain and the course of history can be seen in the words that were imported from French.

1789 *aristocrat*
1790 *sans culottes*
1792 *capitalist, regime, émigré*
1793 *disorganised, demoralised* (meaning *made immoral*), *guillotine*

1795 *terrorism* (meaning *government by terror*)
1797 *tricolore*

And the *tricolore*, as we know, would survive both as a flag and a pizza topping. Moreover, the French contribution to the English language, which had been going on for centuries, would continue for centuries more.

About 30 percent of English words come from French, though it depends, of course, on how you're counting. This means that, though English is basically a Germanic language, we are, at least, one third romantic.

Romance Languages

French is a *romance* language, because the French are, by definition, *romantic*.

Once upon a time there was a thing called the Roman empire that was ruled by Romans in Rome. However, the language they spoke was not called Roman; it was called Latin.

The Roman empire was a grand affair. They had lots of great authors, like Virgil and Ovid, who wrote books in Latin. They also had a frighteningly efficient army that spread death and Latin to every part of the known world.

But empires fall and languages change. Six hundred

years ago, Chaucer could write "al besmotered with his haber-geon," but it's difficult today to make out what he meant, unless you've studied Chaucerian English.

The same thing happened to the Romans and their Latin. There was no sudden break, but little by little their language changed, until nobody in Rome could understand the great Roman authors any more, unless they had studied Latin at school. Slowly, people had to start distinguishing the old Latin from the language that people were speaking on the streets of Rome, which came to be known as *Romanicus*.

The Dark Ages darkened and the difference between Latin and Romanicus grew larger and larger. Latin was pre-served in a way. Classical Latin, or something very like it, became the language of the Catholic Church and of aca-demic discourse. If you wanted to write something that would be taken seriously by a pope or a professor you had to do so in Latin. Even as late as 1687, Isaac Newton still needed to call his great work *Philosophiae Naturalis Principia Mathematica* and publish it in Latin.

Yet in the Middle Ages, most people didn't want to read books about theoretical theology. They wanted stories about knights in shining armour and beautiful damsels in distress. They wanted fire-breathing dragons, enchanted mountains and fairylands beyond the oceans. So such stories got writ-ten by the bucketful, and they were *romanice scribere*, that is to say they were *written in Romanic* (the *–us* had been dropped by this stage).

Not all versions of Romanic were the same. There was the Romanic that had developed in Rome, another one in

France, another in Spain, another in Romania. But *Romanic* became the catchall term for all these languages and then for all the stories that were written in them.

Then lazy people stopped pronouncing the *i* in *Romanic* and the stories and the languages in which they were written stopped being *Romanic* and started to be *romances*.

And that's why, to this day, stories of brave, handsome knights and distressed damsels are called *romances*; and when somebody tries to reproduce the atmosphere of such a tale by taking moonlit walks or lighting candles at dinner, or remembering birthdays, they are being *romantic* or *Roman*.

Peripatetic Peoples

One word that has absolutely nothing to do with *Roman*, *romance* or *Romania* is *Romany*. The people who have for centuries travelled around Europe in caravans have had an awful lot of names, and all of them are insanely inaccurate. The most common name given to them by suspicious house-dwellers is *gypsy*, a name that derives from the utterly false idea that they are from E*gypt*.

Gypsy and *Egyptian* used to be completely interchangeable words. Shakespeare, in *Antony and Cleopatra*, refers to Cleopatra's "gypsy lust" in the very first speech. So where did this idea come from?

The Romany ended up being called Egyptians because of

a single event in 1418, when a band of them arrived in Augsburg claiming to be from "Little Egypt." What exactly they meant by this is unclear, but they wanted money and safe conduct, which was given to them by the authorities and then denied them by the people. The Egyptian idea caught on, and a legend grew up that the Roma were cursed to wander the Earth because when Joseph, Mary and Jesus were obliged to escape the wrath of Herod by fleeing to Egypt, a local tribe had denied them food and shelter. The gypsies, it was reasoned, were the descendants of this tribe, condemned to suffer the same fate for all eternity.

In fact, the Roma are not from Egypt but from India. We know this because their language is more closely related to Sanskrit and Hindi than to anything else. The word *Roma* comes from *Rom*, their word for *man*, which derives ultimately from *domba*, a Sanskrit term for a kind of musician.

That hasn't stopped the legends of their origin spreading, though. The Egyptian mistake has been perpetuated in Hungary, where they were known as *Pharaoh-Nepek*, or *Pharaoh's people*. But different countries have different legends and names, all of which are untrue. In Scandinavia they were thought to be from Tartary and were called the *Tatars*; in Italy it was Walachia and *Walachians*.

The Spanish believed that the Romany were Flemish Belgians. Why they thought this is something of a mystery. Most of the other European mistakes were at least based on the idea that the Roma had come from somewhere eastern and exotic. Indeed, one theory runs that the Spanish were only joking. Whatever the reasoning, the Spanish started to call both the Roma and their style of music Flemish, or *Flamenco*.

The French thought that they must come from Bohemia (now the Czech Republic) and called them *Bohemians*. Then, in 1851, a penniless Parisian writer called Henri Murger came to write about life in the city's Latin Quarter. He decided that the scorn that most of his fellow artists felt for convention made them social Bohemians. So he called his novel *Scènes de la vie de bohème*. The word caught on. Thackeray used it in *Vanity Fair*, and Puccini took Murger's book and turned it into an opera called *La Bohème*. And that's why unconventional and insolvent artists are known to this day as *Bohemians*.

From Bohemia to California (via Primrose Hill)

Bohemia holds a special place in literary geography. The third scene of the third act of Shakespeare's *The Winter's Tale* occurs upon the shores of Bohemia. Indeed, the first line makes sure of it:

Thou art perfect, then, our ship has touched
Upon the deserts of Bohemia?

What is so special about that? Well, let's jump forward by a century and quote *Tristram Shandy*:

> . . . and there happening throughout the whole kingdom
> of Bohemia to be no sea-port town whatever—
> —How the deuce should there, Trim? cried my uncle
> Toby; for Bohemia being totally inland, it could have
> happened no otherwise.
> —It might, said Trim, if it had pleased God.

Whether or not it pleased God, the fallacious notion that Bohemia isn't landlocked pleased Shakespeare, and Bohemia gained in fiction what it never had in fact. Never? Well, almost never. Uncle Toby doesn't seem to know that Bohemia did get a tiny bit of territory on the coast of the Adriatic for a short period in the late thirteenth century, and again in the early sixteenth.

Shakespeare almost certainly didn't know that Bohemia had ever been anything other than landlocked. Shakespeare didn't give a damn about geography. In *The Tempest*, Prospero is abducted from his palace in Milan and bundled down to the docks under cover of darkness. Seventy-four miles overnight is a good bit of bundling in the days before the Ferrari. Not that that bothered the Bard. He had people sailing from Verona and a sail-maker working in Bergamo, an Italian town that's over a hundred miles from the nearest port.

Writers these days devote their time to research, Shakespeare devoted his to writing. He set a whole play in Venice, apparently unaware that there were any canals there; at least he never mentions any, and whenever the city pops up he refers to it as a *land*, even though it's in the sea.

Shakespeare seems never to have consulted a map, and anybody who feels too sniffy about that can, like Cleopatra, go and hang themselves from the top of the pyramids. After all, fiction is only fact minus time. If the polar ice caps keep melting the sea will, eventually, come to Verona, to Milan and finally to Bergamo. Then the Sun will expand and the Earth, in a few billion years' time, will be a parched and burning rock, and the charred bones of Shakespeare, resting in their grave, will be vindicated because all the canals in Venice will be dry.

The poet A. E. Housman took the same attitude with his poem "Hughley Steeple." In a letter to his brother he wrote:

> I ascertained by looking down from Wenlock Edge that Hughley Church could not have much of a steeple. But as I had already composed the poem and could not invent another name that sounded so nice, I could only deplore that the church at Hughley should follow the bad example of the church at Brou, which persists in standing on a plain after Matthew Arnold said [in a poem called "The Church at Brou"] that it stands among mountains.

A French playwright called Alfred de Vigny once wrote a play set in London about the doomed poet Chatterton. Apparently it's a rather good play if you're French, but any Londoner is bound to snigger when Chatterton's friends set off to hunt wild boar on Primrose Hill, which is a small park in a rather leafy little suburb. However, Primrose Hill adjoins London Zoo, so it would only take a loose railing or two to render de Vigny right, and Londoners endangered.

Under the tutelage of time, nonsense becomes geography. The Greeks believed in a country called *Amazonia* filled with fierce female warriors that never existed. Then, a couple of thousand years later, an explorer called Francisco de Orellana was attacked by angry women during a voyage up a big South American river, so he called it the *Amazon*. Or take the case of the utterly fictional island of *California*.

California

The first description of California was written in Spain in about 1510, which is odd because, at the time, no European had been to the western coast of the Americas. But fiction usually beats fact to the punch.

The description was written by Garci Rodriguez de Montalvo, and the reason that he was able to write it with such authority was that California was an entirely fictional place.

Montalvo wrote and compiled stories of high and wonderful chivalry. He had knights in gleaming armour, dragons, sorcerers, maidens in distress, and wonderful exotic locations that he populated with fantastic creatures. In his fourth book, the *Exploits of Esplandian*, he invented a strange island that was near to the lost Garden of Eden.*

Montalvo wrote:

Know that on the right hand from the Indies exists an island called California very close to a side of the Earthly Paradise; and it was populated by black women, without any man existing there, because they lived in the way of the Amazons. They had beautiful and robust bodies, and were brave and very strong. Their island was the strongest of the World, with its cliffs and rocky shores. Their weapons were golden and so were the harnesses of the wild beasts that they were accustomed to domesticate and ride, because there was no other metal in the island than gold.

This gives you some idea of Montalvo's imagination, and also of why the promise of these strong-bodied, sex-starved ladies might have appealed to the lusty Spanish explorers who were sailing off to the New World. We know that Christopher Columbus' son owned a copy of Montalvo's

---

*Just to keep you informed, the Garden of Eden, being perfect, was assumed not to have been destroyed in Noah's flood, but to have been washed far away to some inaccessible place where it could no longer be found.

work, and Cortés, the first European to enter the Pacific, referred to it in a letter of 1524. What's more, the place we now call California was thought to be an island at the time.

Of course, California was never actually an island, but owing to a mistake by an exploratory monk, European map-makers believed that it *was* an island from the sixteenth century up until about 1750. How the explorers got it so wrong is unclear,* but as late as 1716 an English geographer was able to write:

> *California*
> This Island was formerly esteem'd a peninsula, but now found to be intirely surrounded by Water.

Which is good enough for me, and it was good enough for the Spaniards who were deciding what to name this temperate paradise. The explorers decided to name it after the magical land of ferocious (and attractive) women who had appeared in Montalvo's chivalric fantasy.

Montalvo called his island *California* because it was ruled by a beautiful queen called *Calafia*. In the *Exploits of Esplandian*, Calafia has been persuaded to bring her army of ferocious (and attractive) women, plus some trained griffins,

---

*I refer the curious reader to Seymour Schwartz's *The Mismapping of America*, whose detailed account of the mistake I have tried, and failed, to compress.

to fight alongside Muslims and against Christians at the siege of Constantinople. However, Calafia falls in love with Esplandian, is defeated, taken prisoner and converts to Christianity. Then she returns to the island of California with her Spanish husband and her trained griffins.

There are several theories as to why Montalvo chose the name *Calafia*, but by far the most convincing is that, as she was fighting alongside Muslims, her name was chosen to suggest or echo the title of the Muslim leader: the *Caliph*. So California is really, ultimately, etymologically the last surviving *Caliphate*.

The Caliphate, a sometimes factual and sometimes formal union of all Islamic states, was abolished by the Young Turks of Turkey in 1924. Recently there have been strenuous and violent attempts to revive the Caliphate by Al Qaeda. However, if a troop of crack etymologists could be sent into terrorist strongholds, they could gently explain that the Caliphate never disappeared: it's alive and well and is, in fact, the most populous state in America.

The Hash Guys

Even without California complicating the matter, the question of who should be Caliph and what counts as the Caliphate has been a tricky one ever since the Prophet Mohammed died. The first *khalifa* was a fellow called Abu Bakr who had been one of the first converts to Islam. However, after a few years, some folk decided that it shouldn't have gone to him and that the position should, instead, have been handed down to Mohammed's son-in-law and thence to his grandson and so on and so forth from one eldest son to the next. These people were called the Shia, and the others were called the Sunni.

However, heredity in principle always leads to dispute in practice, and so in 765 A.D., when one of the descendants of Mohammed disinherited his eldest son, Ismail, the Shias themselves split into two. There were those who agreed that Ismail should be passed over and there were those who didn't. These latter were called the Ismailis.

The Ismailis did rather well for themselves. They managed, in the ninth century, to conquer most of North Africa and they sent out lots of undercover evangelists to the rest of the Islamic world. These evangelists converted people in secret until there was a huge network of secret Ismailis who were, perhaps, going to help to establish an Ismaili Caliphate once and for all.

But they didn't, because the Sunnis invaded North Africa, burnt all the Ismaili books and converted everybody straight back to the first form of Islam at the point of a scimitar. Now all the Sunnis needed to do was to root out the Ismaili converts in their home territory and everything would be fine and dandy.

So the Ismailis had a hard time of it. They were tracked down and persecuted and fined and put to death and all the other lovely things that mankind likes to do to his neighbour. They couldn't fight the persecution because, though there were a lot of them, they were scattered about here and there and couldn't raise an army. Then an Ismaili called Hasan-i Sabbah had a brilliant idea.

He seized one single, solitary castle near the Caspian Sea. It wasn't a strategically important castle, as it was at the top of a remote mountain at the end of a remote mountain valley in a remote region. But for all these reasons the castle of Alamut was essentially invincible and unattackable. From this base Hasan let it be known that if any Ismailis got persecuted he would respond: not by fighting the soldiers or taking territory or anything like that—he would simply send one of his disciples out to kill the one man, the senior official who had ordered the persecution; and what's more, the killing would be done with a golden dagger.

And they did. The first chap they killed was the Vizier of the Caliphate himself, and then they picked people off left, right and centre. Two things (other than the gold dagger) made them utterly terrifying. The first was that they would get into their target's entourage as sleeper agents and were prepared to work for years as stable boy or servant just to get close enough to the victim. You could hire bodyguards, but how did you know the bodyguards weren't killers themselves? The second was that they were quite prepared to suffer death afterwards; indeed they saw it as a bit of a bonus. They would kill their targets and then kill themselves, confident in the promise of paradise.

Nobody knew what to make of them, but the general

opinion was that they were all on hashish. This is almost certainly untrue, but the name stuck. They were the *hash guys*, or in the colloquial Arabic plural, the *hashshashin*.

Religious fervour fades but gold always gleams, and when the Crusaders arrived in the Middle East they made contact with the Syrian branch of the Ismailis, in a second mountain fortress that was run by the Old Man of the Mountain. The Old Man agreed to hire out the services of his disciples to the Christian invaders, who were immensely impressed by their fatal fanaticism and discipline. Stories of the hash-shashin got back to Europe, where the Arabic H was dropped and the hash guys became the *assassins*.

It wasn't long before *assassin* had been verbed into *assassinate*, and then all you needed was William Shakespeare to invent the word *assassination* for his play *Macbeth*:

> If it were done when 'tis done, then 'twere well
> It were done quickly: if the assassination
> Could trammel up the consequence, and catch
> With his surcease success . . .

But, etymologically speaking, assassination will always be the *cannabisation* of the victim, or the *marijuanafication* or the *potification*, or whatever synonym you want to use for dope.

Drugs

Dope is a terrible thing, and is particularly bad for race-horses. Drug a racehorse just a little bit and you ruin his performance, which is why it's absolutely necessary for a betting man to know in advance which horses have been doped and which are clean-living and ready to win. Such a gambler is said to *have the dope on* a race: the inside knowledge of which runner has *gone to pot*.

Pot itself has nothing to do with pots and pans, but comes from the Mexican-Spanish word *potiguaya*, which means marijuana leaves. And *marijuana* is a Mexification of *Mary Jane* for reasons that everybody is much too stoned to remember. Another Mexican part of drug language is *reefer*, which comes from *grifo*, a word for a drug addict south of the border.

In fact, the vocabulary of drugs is as exotic as their origins. The assassins would, if they did smoke hashish, have done so through a *hookah*, a small pot through which the intoxicating vapours are allowed to bubble. When American troops took up doing the same thing during the Vietnam War, they took the local Thai word for a hookah, *buang*, and turned it into *bong*.

Of course, the terminology of drugs is a matter of dispute, legend and stoned supposition. Nobody is *utterly* sure whether a joint is something smoked in an opium *joint*, or whether it's something that's shared and therefore is *jointly* owned. Nor does anybody have any idea why people from

1920s New Orleans called joints *muggles*, but it sheds an interesting new light on the Harry Potter novels (another of Rowling's characters is called *Mundungus*, which is an archaic word for low-grade tobacco). Whoever invented the word *spliff* didn't bother to write down why.

Dope itself was originally a kind of thick sauce called *doop* into which Dutch people would *dip* pieces of bread. The sense transferred over to drugs only when people started smoking a thick and gloopy preparation of opium. Given that Amsterdam's dope cafes have now become famous throughout the world, it's a little disappointing that any high you might receive from the original Dutch *doop* would be a placebo effect.

Pleasing Psalms

Placebo is Latin for *I will please*, and its origins are not medical, but religious.

From the beginning of the nineteenth century a *placebo* has been a medical term for a "medicine adapted more to please than to benefit the patient." Before this, a *placebo* was any commonplace cure that could be dreamt up by a barely qualified medic. The point was not that that pill would please, but that the doctor would. For long before *placebo* medicines there was *Dr. Placebo*.

In 1697, a doctor called Robert Pierce recalled rather bitterly how he was always being beaten to new business by a charming and talentless medic whose name he was either too polite or too scared to write down. He called him instead *Doctor Placebo*, and noted with tragic jealousy that Placebo's "wig was deeper than mine by two curls."

Whoever the original Dr. Placebo was, his nickname was taken up by various other embittered doctors of the eighteenth century, until *placebo doctors* had given *placebo pills* with *placebo effects*.

At this point things get a little misty, because although *placebo* does mean *I will please*, the word was originally associated not with cures, but with funerals. There's nothing so much fun as a good funeral, and anybody who's truly fond of a good party will tell you that the death rate is much too low, even though it adds up to 100 percent in the end. The drink doled out at a wake has a certain morbid lavishness to it that is rarely or never found at christenings.

People probably still do turn up at the funerals of those they never knew, just in order to get their hands on some booze, but the practice was much more common in medieval times. People would put on their best clothes and turn up to the funerals of the rich, taking part in the service in the hope of joining in the wake.

This meant that they would all stand silent while the first nine verses of Psalm 114 were sung. Then, as it was an antiphon, and as they all wanted to seem particularly enthusiastic about the deceased, they would lustily sing the ninth verse back to the presiding priest:

Placebo Domino in regione vivorum

Which means:

I will please the Lord in the land of the living

In the *Ayenbite of Inwit* ("The Prick of Conscience") from the mid-fourteenth century, the author observes that "the worst flattery is that one that singeth placebo." Chaucer chimes in by saying that "Flatterers [are] the Devil's chaplains that singeth ever Placebo."

So the psalm led to the funeral, which led to the flatterers, which led to the flattering doctors, which led to the placebo pill.

This may all seem rather unlikely, and some etymologists are more inclined to go straight to the Latin *I will please*, but the psalms were much more important in the Middle Ages than they are today, and they have given us all sorts of words that we might not expect. *Memento* became famous because it was the first word of Psalm 131:

Memento Domine David et omnis mansuetudinis eius

Lord, remember David and all his afflictions

Even more obscure is the connection between the psalms and the phrase *to pony up* or pay.

Consider that March 25 is the end of the first quarter of the year, and was thus the first payday for those who were paid quarterly. March 25 was therefore a good day for everybody except employers, and nobody likes them anyway.

People would wake up on March 25, toddle along to church for Matins and sing the psalm with avaricious expectation in their heart. The psalm for that day is the fifth division of Psalm 119, which is the longest psalm in the Bible and needs to be broken up into bite-size chunks. The fifth division begins with the words:

> Legem pone mihi Domine viam iustificationum tuarum et exquiram eam semper

> Teach me, oh Lord, the way of thy statutes; and I shall keep it unto the end

Legem pone therefore became a slang word for a down payment, because in the psalm-obsessed medieval mind it was the first two words of payday. In the centuries since then, the *legem* has been dropped, but that doesn't mean that the phrase has disappeared. If you have ever been asked to *pony up*, it's only a corruption of *legem pone* and a reference to the praises of pay.

Biblical Errors

Some people say that the Bible is the revealed word of God, which would imply that God spoke English. There's even a society in America that believes the King James Version was given to mankind by divine revelation, and it has a big ceremony once a year in which other versions of the Bible are piled up and burnt.

It's certainly true that the King James Version was a lot more accurate than Myles Coverdale's attempt of a hundred years before. Myles Coverdale was an early Protestant who believed in principle that the Bible should be translated into English. He decided that, as nobody else seemed to be doing it, he had better get on with the job himself, and he didn't let the tiny detail that he knew no Latin, Greek or Hebrew get in his way. This is the kind of can-do attitude that is sadly lacking in modern biblical scholarship.

Coverdale did know a bit of German, though, and the Germans, who had invented Protestantism, had already started preparing their own translation. Coverdale threw himself into his work and produced a Psalter that is still used in Church of England services today. It is, though, much more beautiful than it is accurate. For example, he has the line:

> The strange children shall fail: and be afraid out of their prisons.

It's beautiful and mysterious. Who are the strange children? What's so strange about them? And what on earth are they doing in prison? The answer is that the line should be translated as:

> The foreign-born shall obey: and come trembling from their strongholds.

But the best of Coverdale's mistranslations is about Joseph, whose neck, we are told in Psalm 105, was bound in iron. The problem is that Hebrew uses the same word for *neck* as it does for *soul*. The word is *nefesh*, and it usually means *neck* or *throat*, but it can mean *breath* (because you breathe through your neck), and it can also mean *soul*, because the soul is the breath of life. (You have the same thing in Latin and English with *spirit* and *respiratory*.)

If Coverdale had made only one mistake, English would have been given the phrase, *His soul was put in iron*. But Coverdale was never a man to make one mistake when two would do; so he mixed up the subject and the object and came up with the wonderfully inappropriate and nonsensical: *The iron entered into his soul*.

And yet somehow that phrase works. It may have nothing to do with the original Hebrew, but Coverdale's phrase was so arresting that it caught on. Nobody cared that it was a mistranslation. It sounded good.

Even if the translation of the Bible gets it right, English-speakers can still get it wrong. *Strait*, these days, is usually used to describe a narrow stretch of water like the *Bering Straits* or the *Straits of Gibraltar*, but, if you think about it, other things can be *strait*. *Straitjackets* are small jackets used to tie up lunatics. People who are too tightly laced-up are *straitlaced*. If a gate is hard to get through, then it's a *strait gate*, and the hardest gate to pass through is the gate that leads to heaven:

> Because strait is the gate, and narrow is the way, which leadeth unto life, and few there be that find it.

Which is why it's not *the straight and narrow* but *the strait and narrow*.

Finally, *the salt of the earth* is a biblical phrase that has managed to almost reverse its meaning. These days, the salt of the earth are the common folk, the working men and women, the ordinary Joes on the Clapham omnibus; but if that were the case, then the earth would be much too salty to taste good.

When Jesus invented the phrase *the salt of the earth*, he meant exactly the opposite. The world was filled with sinners and pagans, and the only reason that God didn't destroy it utterly was that the few people who believed in Him were like salt to earth's stew.

> Ye are the salt of the earth: but if the salt have lost his savour, wherewith shall it be salted? it is thenceforth good for nothing, but to be cast out, and to be trodden under the foot of men.

This is strange, as Jesus was later crucified by a bunch of Roman *salt-men*.

Salt

Nobody is certain where the word *soldier* comes from, but the best guess is that it has to do with salt. Salt was infinitely more valuable in the ancient world than it is today. To the Romans, salt was white, tasty gold. Legionaries were given a special stipend just to buy themselves salt and make their food bearable; this was called the *salarium* and it's where we get the English word *salary*, which is really just *salt-money*. The Roman writer Pliny the Elder therefore went so far as to theorise that *soldier* itself derived from *sal dare*, meaning *to give salt*. There's nothing intrinsically wrong with this theory, but as Pliny the Elder was a little bit of a nutjob, it should probably be taken with a *pinch of salt*, which, like the salt of the earth, makes something easier to swallow.

Mainly, though, salt is not military but culinary. Salt gets into almost every food, and into an awful lot of food words. The Romans put salt into every single one of their sauces and called them *salsa*. The Old French dropped the L and made this *sauce*, and they did the same with Roman *salsicus*, or salted meats, that turned into *saucisses* and then into *sausages*. The Italians and Spanish kept the L and still make *salami*,* which they can dip into *salsa*, and the Spanish then invented a saucy dance of the same name.

So necessary is salt to a good meal that we usually put it on the table twice. The Old French used to make do with a *salier* or *salt-box* on the table at mealtimes. The English, who are always trying to work out how the French make such delicious food, stole the invention and took it back home.

---

*The Spanish call theirs *salchichón*, which clearly shows the link to *salsicus*.

However, once the *salier* had been removed from France, people quickly forgot the word's origin and how it should be spelt. So we ended up changing *salier* to *cellar*. Then, just to be clear what was in the cellar, we added *salt* onto the beginning and called it a *salt cellar*, which is, etymologically, a *salt-salier* or *salt-salter*.

The Romans would have used a *salt-salter* to season their vegetables and make *herba salata*, which we have since shortened to *salad*. This brings us to a strangely salty coincidence involving the good old days. In *Antony and Cleopatra* the Egyptian queen talks of her

> salad days,
> When I was green in judgment . . .

And the phrase has now taken up residence in the language. We use *salad days* as a synonym for *halcyon days*, which by an odd coincidence also means *salty days*.

Halcyon Days

People talk nostalgically of the halcyon days. They hanker and pine, and in the midst of their hankering they ask if we shall ever see such halcyon days again.

We shall.

The Halcyon Days begin each year on December 14 and

last until the 28, and like the salad days they are, etymologically, very salty. This time the salt is Greek, and so the prefix we're looking for is *hal–*, the same *hal,* in fact, that you find in the salt-producing chemicals known as *halo*gens.

Indeed, halcyon and halogen are etymologically almost identical: the one gives birth to salt, the other is a salty conception. That's because *halcyon* is another word for the kingfisher, and kingfishers lay their eggs at sea.

For a full and accurate explanation of all this, we shall have to turn to the Roman poet Ovid, who explained it all in his *Metamorphoses.* Once upon a time there was a boy called Ceyx and a girl called Halcyon who fell madly in love. Unfortunately, Ceyx had to go away to sea and Halcyon would wait for him every day on the beach, gazing at the horizon and longing for her lover's return.

Halcyon continued this vigil until she was informed, by the utterly reliable medium of a dream, that Ceyx's ship had sunk and he had been drowned. At this news she got so upset that she fell ill and died a couple of days later; or, as Chaucer put it in one of his most beautiful couplets:

Alas! She said for very sorrow
And died within the thridde morrow.

Everybody was very upset by the whole business including the gods, who got together and decided that the least they could do for the poor couple was to turn them into birds. So Ceyx and Halcyon were raised from the dead and covered in feathers, and that's where kingfishers come from.

Because Halcyon had spent so long gazing out to sea, that's where she now lays her eggs in a little floating nest; and, just to make sure she's not disturbed, the gods have arranged that the winds should be light during her nesting season, which lasts through the second half of December. This fortnight of good weather is therefore known as the Halcyon Days.

Of course, modern biologists scoff at Ovid's story and dismiss it purely on the basis that it isn't true. However, poetry is much more important than truth, and, if you don't believe that, try using the two methods to get laid.

Dog Days

The Dog Days, like the Halcyon ones, are a precisely defined part of the year, or at least they were once. The second brightest star in the sky (after the Sun) is Sirius, the Dog Star, so called because it's the largest star in the Great Dog constellation, Canis Major. However, during the height of summer you can't see the Dog Star because it rises and sets at the same time as the Sun. The ancient Greeks worked out that this happened from July 24 to August 24, and they noticed that this was also the most unpleasantly hot time of the year. So they, quite logically, decided that it must be the combined rays of the Sun and the Dog Star that were causing the trouble. They also thought a lot about how to cool down. The ancient Greek writer Hesiod has this advice:

> In the season of wearisome heat, then goats are plump-
> est and wine sweetest; women are most wanton, but men
> are feeblest, because Sirius parches head and knees and
> the skin is dry through heat. But at that time let me have
> a shady rock and wine of Biblis, a clot of curds and milk
> of drained goats with the flesh of an heifer fed in the
> woods, that has never calved, and of firstling kids; then
> also let me drink bright wine, sitting in the shade, when
> my heart is satisfied with food, and so, turning my head
> to face the fresh Zephyr, from the everflowing spring
> which pours down unfouled, thrice pour an offering of
> water, but make a fourth libation of wine.

It's well worthwhile memorising that passage and reciting it to a waiter on the first of the Dog Days. However, you must be careful, as, owing to the precession of the equinoxes, the Dog Days have slowly shifted over the last two thousand years and now begin around July 6, although it depends on your latitude.

None of this has anything whatsoever to do with the notion that every dog will have his day, which comes from *Hamlet*:

> Let Hercules himself do what he may,
> The cat will mew and dog will have his day.

We call it the Dog Star, the Romans called it *Canicula* (meaning *dog*)* and the Greeks called it *Sirius*, which meant *scorching*, because of the heat of the Dog Days. However, the Greeks also sometimes referred to it as *Cyon* (the Dog), and the star that rises just before Sirius is still called *Procyon*; and that same Greek word for dog—*cyon*—also gave the English language the word *cynic*.

Cynical Dogs

The Cynics were a school of ancient Greek philosophy, founded by Antisthenes and made famous by his pupil Diogenes.

Diogenes was, by any standards, an odd chap. He lived in a barrel in the marketplace in Athens and used to carry a lamp about in broad daylight, explaining that he was trying to find an honest man. His one worldly possession was a mug that he used for drinking. Then one day he saw a peasant scooping water up with his hands and immediately threw his mug away. Accounts of his death vary, but one story is that he held his breath.

Cynic meant *doglike*. But why was Diogenes' school known as *the dogs*?

---

*The French still call a heatwave *une canicule*.

There was a *gymnasium* near Athens for those who were not of pure Athenian blood. A gymnasium in ancient Greece wasn't exactly the same thing as a gymnasium today. For starters, it was an open-air affair. It was more of a leafy glade than a building filled with parallel bars and rubber mats. People did do their physical training at the gymnasium; in fact, they did it naked. The word *gymnasium* comes from the Greek *gymnazein*, meaning *to train in the nude*, which itself comes from *gymnos*, meaning *naked*. But if you could take your mind off the naked boys (which many Greek philosophers found difficult), gymnasiums were also places for socialising and debating and teaching philosophy. Diogenes' gymnasium was known as the Gymnasium of the White Dog or *Cynosarge*, because a white dog had once defiled a sacrifice there by running away with a bit of meat.

Diogenes, not being a native Athenian, was forced to teach in the Dog's Gymnasium, which is how one hungry and ownerless canine gave his name to a whole philosophical movement. A fun little result of this is that any cynical female is, etymologically speaking, a bitch.

Greek Education and Fastchild

If Cynics are dogs, the Stoics were the *porch philosophers* because their founder Zeno taught in the painted porch or *Stoa Poikile* of the Great Hall in Athens. If you didn't like either the Stoics or the Cynics you could go out to a grove that was named after a hero of the Trojan War called *Akademos*. It was in the grove of *Akademeia* that Plato taught, and all *academies* since are named after it, which means that the *Police Academy* films are all named after a hero of the Trojan War via Plato.

The Athenians, as you can tell, were jolly philosophical chaps. This was largely because they had a wonderful education system in which the Greek children, or *paedos*, were taken through the whole cycle, or *cyclos*, of learning. Their knowledge was therefore *en-cyclo-paedic*.

The Romans were so impressed with the way Greek children were taught all these different subjects that they started writing books called *encyclopaedias* that were meant to contain articles on every topic there was. Then, two thousand years later, the internet was invented.

The internet works on computers, and computers work on all sorts of different programming languages. These programming languages tend to be rather complicated things that are hard to learn and, even for initiates, slow to use. So in 1994 a chap called Ward Cunningham developed a system of making related webpages that would be very simple and very fast. Because it was so quick, he called it *wikiwiki-web*, because *wiki* is Hawaiian for *fast* and the reduplication *wikiwiki* therefore means *very fast indeed*.

Soon, though, people decided that *wikiwiki* was a bit of a mouthful, and so it was colloquially shortened to *wiki*. That was the state in which Larry Sanger found the word in 2001, when he had the idea of a collaborative, web-based encyclopaedia that would use the wiki system. He took the words *wiki* and *encyclopedia* and mashed them together to form *Wikipedia*, which is now the seventh most visited website in the world. However, few among its 365 million readers know that *Wikipedia* means *Fastchild*. Fewer still will have considered the fact that anyone who likes Wikipedia is technically and etymologically a *Wikipedophile*.

Cybermen

These days, if you aren't *wiki* or *cyber* or *virtual*, you are nothing. You might as well give up and make do with real life, which mankind has been trying for thousands of years without success.

Cyberspace is out of control and filled with cybersquatters having cybersex with cyberpunks. This would make more sense if anybody actually knew what *cyber* meant, and the answer may come as a shock to cyberpunks, because *cyber* means *controlled*—indeed, it comes from the same root as *governed*.

Back in the 1940s there was a man called Norbert Wiener who was studying how animals and machines communicated with and controlled each other. He decided to call his field of study *cybernetics* after the Greek word for a steersman. A steersman controls the boat that he's in: in Greek, he *cubernans* it. From this the Romans got the idea that a governor who steers the ship of state *gubernans* it. Even though the B has been replaced by a V in the modern *governor*, things that belong to the governor are still *gubernatorial*.

Meanwhile, *punk* was an early twentieth-century American term for a homosexual, specifically the young and pliable companion of an elderly and implacable hobo. From there, *punk* turned into a generalised insult and then was taken as a badge of honour by noisy rockers in the 1970s. However, an etymologist can still look at the term *cyberpunk* and wonder what these well-governed homosexuals are up to.

Another word that has switched its meaning entirely is *virtual*. Virtual reality, in case you didn't know, is reality that isn't real. It's *virtually real*, though that's not much better than being *virtually pregnant*. But what really bothers the etymologist is that very few of the things that happen in virtual reality are in the slightest bit *virtuous*.

If one thing is *virtually* another, it's because it shares the same *virtues*. Of course, *virtues* here don't have to be moral virtues, they can be physical ones. If I'm virtually asleep, then I'm not asleep but possess the same physical virtues as somebody who is. A virtue doesn't have to be good: a *virtu*oso torturer isn't a good man, he's just good at his job. It's the sense of virtue that survives in the phrase *by virtue of.*

Even though you can now achieve things *by virtue of dishonesty*, *virtue* used to be a much better thing. Courage, strength, honesty and generosity all used to be virtues, although few of those survive in virtual reality. In the ancient world, a virtue was anything that was commendable in a person. Well, I say person, but I mean man.

Women can't be virtuous. A virtue is *that which is proper to a man*. The Latin for *man* was *vir*, and *virtus* was the Latin word for *manliness*. *Virtue* is basically the same thing as *virility*.

So if a woman were to be virtuous she would become a man-woman, which is a terrible idea. A man-woman might be so bold as to have her own opinions. She might even express them, at which point she would become a *virago*.

To be fair, *virago* was originally a word for a heroic woman; but that's still rather sexist, as it implies that heroism is a purely manly quality. In fact, language is irredeemably sexist; but that's not my fault, it's the Romans.' Look at their attitude to women in the workplace.

Turning Trix

Meretricious is an odd little word that lots of people get wrong. It sounds a little like *merit* and, as merit is a good thing, you would take a guess that *meretricious* means, well, *meritable*.

It doesn't. *Meretricious* means *showy*, *gaudy* and *contemptible*. However, the *meret* in *meretricious* is the same Latin root that you find in *merit*. The only difference is that it's women who are doing the meriting.

When the Romans wanted to point out that somebody was female, they would put a *trix* on the end on the word. It's a habit that has largely died out, but you still find it occasionally. A female aviator is sometimes an *aviatrix*, a female editor can be an *editrix*, and a lady who is paid to dominate men is a *dominatrix*.

There used to be more trixes—a *tonstrix* was a female hairdresser—but they slowly died out. Back in ancient Rome, though, they didn't like women having jobs at all. In fact, almost the only women who had jobs in Rome were the women who stood in front of brothels looking for customers. The Latin for *standing in front* of things is *pro-stitutio*.

It was a way of earning a living, almost the only one for a girl, and the Latin for earning was *merere*. When a man earned a living he *merited* it, and became *meritable*. A veteran soldier who had retired to spend his money could proudly call himself *emeritus*, meaning that he had *earned* all he needed and retired, which is where we get emeritus professors.

That's because a soldier was a man. But when a girl earned a living she was a *meretrix*, and *meretrix* could mean only one thing: tart. And that's why *meretricious* still means *tarty*.

Amateur Lovers

The opposite of *meretricious* can be found hidden away in the game of tennis, where the true nature of love can also be discovered. But first, a brief note on the word *tennis*. It's not called that, you know. The proper term for the game played at Wimbledon is *sphairistike*.

The rules of tennis as we know them were set down by a man called Major Walton Clopton Wingfield back in the 1890s. Tennis had been played before, of course—Shakespeare refers to the game several times—but it had always been played by kings and princes in the courtyards of palaces. It wasn't until the invention of the lawnmower in the nineteenth century that people were able to play on lawns. Major Walton Clopton Wingfield wanted to distinguish his new game from the old tennis, which came from the French word *tenez*, meaning *hold!* So he lighted on the name *sphairistike*, which is ancient Greek for *ball-skill*.

Sphairistike became wildly popular, but there was one hitch: nobody knew how the hell to pronounce it. Did it rhyme with *pike*? Or with *piquet*? In fact, it rhymed with *sticky*, but nobody knew that. So rather than make fools of themselves by getting it wrong, people just decided to call it *lawn tennis* and to hell with Major Walton Clopton Wingfield and his Greek.

Wingfield did keep the scoring system of the old tennis, though, and it's there that we may find the true nature of love. You may have heard that *love* in tennis is a corruption of the French *l'oeuf*, meaning *egg*, because an egg looks a bit like a zero. This is a myth.* *Love* is *nothing* because those who do something for the love of it do it for nothing. For

---

*It is, though, true in cricket, where a zero was referred to as a *duck's egg*, which then got shortened to *duck*.

example, people either marry for money or connections, or for love. Love therefore became a synonym for nothing, because if you do something purely for love, you get nothing. By 1742 this notion of *love* being *zero* had been taken across to games and sports. In fact, the first known reference is to the score in whist.

Love in tennis is therefore the exact opposite of prostitution. It's the celebration of the *amateur*. *Amare* is the Latin for *love*, from which we get *amiable*, *amorous* and *paramour*. And if you were doing something for your paramour, you wouldn't charge for it, would you? As late as 1863, a man could still write that he was "not an amateur of melons," which simply meant that he didn't like them.

The distinction between amateur and professional is merely a distinction between those who love what they do, and those who do it because they are paid. Unfortunately this means that all lovers are rather amateurish. They can't help it, it's built into the etymology.

Love is much better than money. You should be afraid of money—that's what *money* means.

Dirty Money

Money is a monster, etymologically speaking. It all comes down to the Latin word *monere*, and even though the connection is accidental it's probably still significant.

Monere was Latin for *warn*, and if you have a pre-*monition* you are forewarned. In the ancient world they believed that horrible beasts were omens of disasters. The idea was that just before the fall of an emperor or the loss of a great battle, centaurs, griffins and sphinxes would come out of wherever they were hiding and roam around in full view. These unnatural creatures, composed of the parts of other animals, were therefore called *warnings*, or *monsters* (*monstrum*, from *monere*).

However, if you need a warning and can't afford a centaur, geese will do just as well. People still keep guard geese because they kick up a fearsome racket if they spot an intruder and they can also be pretty vicious. You should never say boo to a goose, not unless you're prepared for a fight. The Romans kept guard geese on the Capitoline Hill. This came in useful when Rome was attacked by the Gauls in 390 B.C., so useful, in fact, that the Romans put up a temple in thanksgiving. But being ungrateful sods they didn't dedicate it to geese, they dedicated it to Juno, the goddess of warnings, or *Juno Moneta*.

Next door to the temple of Juno Moneta was the building where all the Roman coins were produced. In fact, the coins may have been made in part of the temple itself. Nobody is quite sure, and the sources are rather vague. What is certain is that the coin-producing building got named after the temple. It was the *Moneta*, and though we've changed all the vowels, we still call such a building a *mint*.

In the Moneta, they produced *moneta*: literally *warnings*. The French took the word and dropped the T so that it was already *money* when it arrived in English. However, our adjective *monetary*, meaning *related to money*, keeps the reference to the temple and the angry geese alive and well.

It's only by an accident of propinquity that *money* is a *monster*. Perhaps you shouldn't worry about it at all. Money's not that bad. You shouldn't be so frightened. Go on, take out that *death pledge*. Sorry: *mortgage*.

Death Pledges

Anyone who has ever taken out a mortgage will be unsurprised to learn that it is, literally, a *death pledge*. However, it's the sort of thing you would only usually notice if you were taking out a mortgage on a *mort*uary. *Mort* is death, and *mort*al man has nothing else waiting for him. Nothing is certain in this life except death and mortgages.

The reason a mortgage is called a death pledge is that it can die in two ways. You can pay off the whole thing, in which case the deal dies and you own your house. However, that happy ending is far from certain in these troubled and impoverished times. The other possibility is that you fail to make a payment, the deal dies, and your house is repossessed. The whole thing was spelt out in *mort*ifying terms in the *Institutes and Laws of England* in 1628:

> It seemeth that the cause why it is called mortgage is, for
> that it is doubtful whether the Feoffor will pay at the day

limited such summe or not, and if he doth not pay, then the Land which is put in pledge vpon condition for the payment of the money, is taken from him for euer, and so dead to him vpon condition, etc. And if he doth pay the money, then the pledge is dead as to the Tenant, etc.

There are a lot of hidden deaths in English. Many people will have noticed the similarity between the words *executive* and *executioner*, but what have the two got in common? Is it that an executioner is just somebody who executes the sentence, just as an undertaker is someone who undertakes to bury you? No. The original legal term for execution was *execute to death*, from the French *exécuter à mort*. So you execute the sentence until they die.

Another hidden *mort* comes in the word *caput*. Monks used to remind themselves of their own mortality by contemplating a skull. This was called a *death's head* or *caput mortuum*, and the original owner of a *caput mortuum* was definitely *caput*. It's enough to make you scream *blue murder*, which is a direct translation of the French phrase *mort bleu*, which itself is a non-blasphemous form of *mort dieu*, or *death of God*.

The *gage* in *mortgage* is much more cheerful. It means *pledge* and is exactly the same *gage* that you find when you fall in love and get *engaged*. It's also very closely related to *waging* war.

Wagering War

You can't really *wage* anything other than *war*. You can try, but it sounds rather odd. Indeed, the phrase *waging war* gets stranger the more you look at it. Does it have anything to do with wages, or wage disputes, or maybe freeing the wage slaves? There's a connection between all these different *wages*, and indeed to *wagers*. But you have to go back to the fourteenth century.

A *wage* was, originally, a *pledge* or *deposit*. *Wage* is simply a different way of pronouncing the *gage* in mort*gage* and en*gage*ment.* A wage was something given in security. From this *wage* you quite easily get to the modern *wager*: it's merely the stake, or deposit, thrown down by a gambler. It's also reasonably simple to see how *money given in security* could end up meaning *money given as pay*. But waging war? That involves trial by combat.

In medieval law it was considered quite reasonable to settle a legal dispute by duelling to the death. Though somebody had to die in this system and there was no guarantee of justice, lawyers' fees were at least kept to a minimum.

A wronged medieval man would throw down his *gage/ wage* (or pledge), and challenge his opponent to trial by combat. In Latin that was *vadiare duellum*; in French it was

---

*The medievals often mixed up their Gs and Ws, which is why another word for *guarantee is warranty*.

gager bataille; in English you *waged* [pledged yourself to] *battle*.

Not war. *Battle*. It was, after all, a technical legal term for the violent resolution of individual arguments. You *wagered* your body in mortal combat. However, it's easy to see how the sense of *waging battle* extended from the promise of violence to the act of violence.

In the end, when two countries couldn't agree, they started *waging war* against each other. This last shift in meaning could reasonably be described as *wage inflation*.

Strapped for Cash

Why are people so often *strapped for cash*?

Being strapped for cash is actually a good thing. If you're falling down and you need something to hang on to, a strap is good. If you fall overboard, it's a good thing if somebody throws you a strap. And if you've fallen from the ship of solvency and are drowning in a sea of debt, then you very much want somebody to throw you a strap. Of course, it means that you're currently in debt, but to be strapped for cash is better than to have no cash at all.

Oddly, the same metaphor has been invented twice. These days, when a bank is about to go bankrupt, the government throws them a *lifeline*. This means that the bank survives, although they are still strapped for cash.

Incidentally, *bank* comes from an old Italian word for *bench*, because money-lenders used to sit behind a bench in the marketplace from which they would do their deals. If a money-lender failed to make good on one of his arrangements, his bench would be ceremonially broken, and the old Italian for a broken bench was *banca-rotta* or *bankrupt*.

Fast Bucks and Dead Ones

So almost every form of money involves death, danger and destruction. A frightened word-lover might start to wish that the stuff had never been invented at all. It is, after all, possible to run a society without any money. America, which is now the land of the *fast buck*, had no money until European colonists arrived.

Well, almost. On the coasts of the Northeast they used clam shells called *wampums* that could be threaded together into necklaces, and in Mexico they used coffee beans as a standard by which to barter; but the point, essentially, stands. There were no coins, no notes, no green and folding pictures of presidents.

This presented a problem to those colonists who wanted to trade. The natives looked on coins and banknotes with a mixture of scorn and confusion. What were they meant to do with that? You couldn't wear it round your neck, you couldn't even make a nice cup of coffee from it.

Early attempts at trading involved tobacco. Tobacco made a lot more sense than coins. With tobacco, the peace pipe could be pulled out, and if you combined it with the coffee beans of Mexico you might feel almost civilised. But of course tobacco needs to be weighed out, and it's rather bulky. The harvests go up and down, causing sudden inflation and deflation, and you need a warehouse to store it in.

So the traders eventually gave up on tobacco and moved to another staple item that everybody knew and valued: deerskins. A deerskin can be slapped over the saddle of a horse, it's thin and light, and when you're not spending it you can use it to keep warm. Buckskins soon became the standard unit of barter in North America, and a standard unit of barter is, in effect, money. So it was buckskins, or *bucks* for short, that were used for trade.

With this in mind, let us turn to Conrad Weiser, the first man ever to *make a buck*. He was born in Germany in 1696, but his family, being Protestant, were forced to flee to Britain in 1709. There they were held in a refugee camp just outside London before being sent to populate the colonies on the Hudson River. In 1712, when Conrad was sixteen, his father took the rather extraordinary step of sending his son to live with the Mohawk tribe for half a year. Conrad learnt the language and the customs of the Iroquois and started an illustrious career as a diplomat for the British among the native tribes of America.

Despite having fourteen children, Conrad still found the time to negotiate most of the significant treaties between the British and the disgruntled tribes and convince them that their real enemies were the French. In 1748 Conrad was sent into Ohio to negotiate with the tribes of the Five Nations. His mission had several purposes. One was to make peace and seek amends after the murder of some colonists. In this he succeeded. The tribal council told him that:

> . . . what was done we utterly abhor as a thing done by the Evil Spirit himself; we never expected any of our People wou'd ever do so to our Brethren [the British]. We therefore remove our Hatchet which, by the influence of the Evil Spirit, was struck into your Body, and we desire that our Brethren the Gov. of New York & Onas may use their utmost endeavours that the thing may be buried in the bottomless Pit.

. . . which is one of the earliest references to *burying the hatchet*. The next item on the agenda, though, was rather more tricky. It involved rum. Specifically, it involved a request that the British would stop selling rum to the Ohio Indians. To this Weiser replied that:

> . . . you never agree about it—one will have it, the other won't (tho' very few), a third says we will have it cheaper; this last we believe is spoken from your Hearts (here they Laughed). Your Brethren, therefore, have order'd that every cask of Whiskey shall be sold to You for 5 Bucks in your Town, & if a Trader offers to sell Whiskey to You and will not let you have it at that Price, you may take it from him & drink it for nothing.

And that is the very first reference to a *buck* as a unit of American currency. The deal was then finalised with a belt of wampum.

This was good news for American trade, but bad news for American deer. However, it was all about to get much worse for the American buck. Not content with their skins, the Americans were about to make a phrase out of their horns.

The Buck Stops Here

You might assume that *passing the buck* has something to do with passing a dollar to the person next to you. This is not so. After all, passing a dollar would hardly shift responsibility to someone. The only thing that these two *bucks* have in common is a dead deer.

Not, of course, that you pass a whole animal. That would be ridiculous. The phrase *to pass the buck* simply involves another part of the buck's corpse.

Deer don't have a good time in language. Their entrails are put into pies and their skins are used in lieu of currency; one of the few parts of the buck deer that remains is the horn. Waste not, want not.

A buck's horn makes a very pleasant-looking knife handle, and a knife has many uses. You can cut up venison with a knife, or you can skin another deer and make a fast buck. You can also use a knife to mark the dealer in a game of poker by stabbing it into the table in front of whoever currently has responsibility for handing round the cards.

This isn't done much by people who value their furniture, but in the Wild West, life and woodwork were cheap, and the first reference to *passing the buck* comes from the diary of a "border ruffian" during the fight for Kansas in 1856. On approaching a place called Buck Creek, he says that "we remembered how gladly would we 'pass' the Buck as at 'poker.' "

This is odd because the dealer usually has a slight advantage in poker. However, among the border ruffians of the Wild West the dealer probably stood a good chance of being shot, as, if you suspect there's cheating going on, the dealer is the first chap you should murder.

So bucks were passed without cease until the 1940s, when they finally stopped in a prison in El Reno, Oklahoma. The prison governor had decided that all responsibility ended with him. He dealt, and the prisoners received. So he had a sign put up in his office saying that "THE BUCK STOPS HERE."

Of course, the buck didn't really stop there. The prison governor had to answer to the state government and then to the federal government and then to the president, with whom the buck would grind to a final and undeniable halt. This point was not lost upon an aide to Harry S. Truman who visited the prison and saw the sign. He liked it so much that he had a replica made. He gave it to President Truman, who put it up in his office and made the phrase famous.

So are all bucks really deer? Almost.

Back to Howth Castle and Environs

So the humble buck-deer is the source of all things *buck*, with one exception. *Buckwheat*, which looks like it should be the wheat that bucks eat, has nothing whatsoever to do with deer.

The leaves of buckwheat look very similar to the leaves of a beech tree. The German for *beech* is *Buche* and so *buckwheat* is really *beechwheat*.

Beech trees were important to the ancient Germans. Beechwood is thick-grained and not splitty (to use woodworking terminology), so it's easy to carve things in it, and that's exactly what the Germans used to do. Beech, *buche* or *bok*, as it was called in Old High German, was the standard material for writing on. Even when wood was finally overtaken by the newfangled invention of parchment, the Germans kept the name, and so did the English. *Bok* became *boc* became *book*.

This is a book. The glorious insanities of the English language mean that you can do all sorts of odd and demeaning things to a book. You can cook it. You can bring a criminal to it, or, if the criminal refuses to be brought, you can throw it at him. You may even take a leaf out of it, the price of lavatory paper being what it is. But there is one thing that you can never do to a book like this. Try as and how you might, you cannot turn up for it. Because a *turn-up for the books* [continued on page 1].

QUIZZES

In Lewis Carroll's book *Through the Looking Glass, and What Alice Found There* (often erroneously referred to as *Alice Through the Looking Glass*), Humpty Dumpty tells Alice: "There's glory for you."

"I don't know what you mean by 'glory,' " Alice said.

Humpty Dumpty smiled contemptuously. "Of course you don't—till I tell you. I meant 'there's a nice knock-down argument for you!' "

"But 'glory' doesn't mean 'a nice knock-down argument,' " Alice objected.

"When I use a word," Humpty Dumpty said, in rather a scornful tone, "it means just what I choose it to mean—neither more nor less."

"The question is," said Alice, "whether you can make words mean so many different things."

However, as the greatest joy a human being can achieve in this sorrowful world is to get one up on his or her fellow man or woman by correcting their English, and as I have spent far too long consulting dictionaries, here's a list of some common English words and what the dictionaries say they actually mean:

Burgeon—To bud

Blueprint—The absolutely final plans that are sent to the factory

Backlash—The small period of inactivity when a system of cogs is reversed

Celibate—Unmarried

Compendium—Brief summary

Condone—Forgive

Coruscate—To glow intermittently

Decimate—To reduce by 10 percent

Enormity—Crime

Effete—Exhausted

Fulsome—Over the top

Jejune—Unsatisfying

Noisome—Annoying

Nauseous—Causing nausea

Pleasantry—Joke

Pristine—Unchanged

Refute—To utterly disprove

Restive—Refusing to move (obviously)

Scurrilous—Obscene

Swathe—The area of grass cut with one stroke of a scythe

As you will have learnt from the preceding stroll through the English language, it's almost impossible to guess where a word has come from or where it's going to go to. So here, just to puzzle you, are a series of quizzes in which you have to guess where a word has come from or where it's going to go to.

We shall start with some names of famous people. Except that I haven't given you the names, I've given you the etymological meaning. So, for example, if I were to write *God of war and man of peace*, the answer would be me, Mark Forsyth, because *Mark* comes from *Mars*, the Roman god of battles, and *Forsyth* is Gaelic for *man of peace*. Got that? Good. Let us begin. (Answers follow.)

POLITICIANS OF THE LAST HUNDRED YEARS
1. Blessed, handsome and crooked (U.S. president)
2. Courageous cabbage (European politician)
3. Noble wolf who lives in a hut (Second World War)
4. God loved the ugly-face (U.S. president)
5. Blessed one from Mosul (Second World War)

MUSIC
1. God loves a mud-caked, travelling wolf (composer; clue: *wolves*)
2. My little French lady (female pop star; clue: *my lady*)
3. Loud war in the vegetable garden (composer; clue: *he wouldn't have heard it anyway*)
4. Tattooed javelin-thrower (female pop star; clue: *another word for javelins*)

5. The dwarf in the priest's garden (male rock star; clue: *middle name Aaron*)

GLAMOUR

1. Victorious goatherd (actress; clue: *baby goat*)
2. Christmas councillor (actress; clue: *odd name as she's Israeli*)
3. Cruel twin (actor; clue: *a kind of missile*)
4. The moon at the ford of blood (supermodel; clue: *----ford*)
5. He who listens among the cows (TV; clue: *cow---*)

WRITERS

1. Little Richard's husband (nineteenth-century novelist)
2. Good Christian (twentieth-century novelist)
3. Virile wonder (seventeenth-century poet)
4. Pants-maker in a peaceful land (fourteenth-century poet)
5. Tiny foreign snake (twentieth-century novelist)

And the answers are:

POLITICIANS OF THE LAST HUNDRED YEARS

1. Blessed, handsome and crooked = **Barack Hussein Obama**

   Barack is Swahili for *blessed*. *Hussein* is Arabic for *handsome*. *Obama* is Dholuo for *crooked*.

2. Courageous cabbage = **Helmut Kohl**

   Nobody is quite sure what the *hel* means, but *mut* is definitely *brave* and *kohl* is *cabbage*.

3. Noble wolf who lives in a hut = **Adolf Hitler**

   Adolf is *edel wolf*, which means *noble wolf*, and so far as anyone can tell, a *hitler* is just somebody who lives in a *hut*.

4. God loved the ugly-face = **JFK**

   John comes from the Latin *Johannes*, which comes from the Hebrew *y'hohanan*, which means *Jahweh has favoured*. *Kennedy* comes from the Irish *O Cinnéide*, which means *ugly head*.

5. Blessed one from Mosul = **Benito Mussolini**

   Benito means *blessed* and *Mussolini* means *muslin*, because his ancestor was probably a merchant who dealt in muslin. However, *muslin—mussolina* in Italian—gets its name from Mosul in Iraq, where it was believed to be made.

MUSIC

1. God loves a mud-caked, travelling wolf = **Wolfgang Amadeus Mozart**

   Wolfgang is German for a *travelling wolf*, *Amadeus* is Latin for *loved* (*ama*) by *god* (*deus*), and *Mozart* comes from the Allemanic *motzen* meaning *to roll about in the mud.* It was originally an insulting term for somebody dirty.

2. My little French lady = **Madonna Ciccone**
   Ma donna is Italian for *my lady*. *Ciccone* is an augmentative of *Cicco*; but *Cicco* is a diminutive of *Francesco*. So it means *little Francis*, and *Francis* means *French*.

3. Loud war in the vegetable garden = **Ludwig van Beethoven**
   Lud means *loud*, *wig* means *war*, and a *beet hoven* is a *garden* that grows the vegetable *beet*.

4. Tattooed javelin-thrower = **Britney Spears**
   Britney was a surname meaning *British*. *Britain* comes from *prittanoi*, which means *the tattooed people*. *Spears* is a shortening of *spearman*.

5. The dwarf in the priest's garden = **Elvis Presley**
   So far as anybody can tell, *Elvis* comes from *Alvis*, a dwarf in Viking mythology. *Presley* is a variant of *Priestly* and means *one who lives on land belonging to a priest*.

GLAMOUR

1. Victorious goatherd = **Nicole Kidman**
   Nicole is the feminine of *Nicholas*. *Nicholas* is from the Greek *nike laos*. *Nike* means victory (as in the sneakers)

and *laos* means people. A *kidman* is a man who looks after the *kid goats*.

2. Christmas councillor = **Natalie Portman**
Natalie is related to *natal* and comes from the day of Jesus' birth, or *dies natalis*. A *portmann* in Old English was a townsman elected to administrate the affairs of a borough.

3. Cruel twin = **Tom Cruise**
Thomas comes from the Semitic *toma*, meaning *twin*, and *Cruise* comes from the Middle English *crus*, meaning *fierce* or *cruel*.

4. The moon at the ford of blood = **Cindy Crawford**
Cindy is a variant of *Cynthia*, which was an epithet of Artemis and meant *moon*. *Craw* or *cru* was Gaelic for *blood*, and *ford* is *ford*.

5. He who listens among the cows = **Simon Cowell**
Simon is often and justifiably confused with the identical ancient Greek name *Simon*, which meant *snub-nosed* (as in *simian*). However, our Christian *Simon* comes from a different root: *Symeon*. It's from the Bible and the Hebrew *shim'on*, which means *listening*. *Cowell* is just *cowfield*.

WRITERS

1. Little Richard's husband = **Charles Dickens**
   Charles is from the German *karl*, which meant either *man* or *husband*. *Dickens* is a diminutive of *Dick*, which is short for *Richard*.

2. Good Christian = **Agatha Christie**
   Agathos was ancient Greek for *good*. *Christie* means Christian.

3. Virile wonder = **Andrew Marvell**
   Andreios was ancient Greek for *manly*. *Marvell* means marvel.

4. Pants-maker in a peaceful land = **Geoffrey Chaucer**
   Geoffrey comes from the Latin *Gaufridus*, which in turn comes from the Old German *gewi*, land, and *fridu*, peaceful. *Chaucer* is from Old French *chaucier*, meaning *man who makes chausses*. *Chausses* could refer to almost anything worn on the lower half of the body.

5. Tiny foreign snake = **Evelyn Waugh**
   Evelyn is a double-diminutive of *Eve*, so it's *tiny Eve*. In the Bible, *Eve—hawah*—is said to come from Hebrew *havah, she who lived*; however, this looks rather like a folk etymology and the word is suspiciously similar to *haya*, which is Aramaic for *serpent*.

Waugh probably comes from *wahl*, which is the Old English for *foreigner*.

Now, a quick trip around the capital cities of the world. Can you make out the modern names from the original meanings? For example, if I were to say *Place of the Bad Smell*, you would immediately realise that I was referring to the Objibwa *Shika Konk*, which developed into our *Chicago*. To make it guessable, we shall stick to capital cities.

Europe
Merchant harbour
Place by an unfordable river
Wisdom
Smoky bay
Black pool

Africa
Three cities
Victorious
New flower
The place of cool waters
End of an elephant's trunk

Asia
Muddy confluence
Modern

Garden
Anchor
Father of a gazelle

The Americas
Good winds
I saw a mountain
Peace
Place of many fish
Traders

And the answers are:

Europe
Merchant harbour—Copenhagen
Place by an unfordable river—London
Wisdom—Sofia (although Athens is named after Athena,
    goddess of wisdom, so give yourself half a pat on the
    back for that)
Smoky bay—Reykjavik
Black pool—Dublin

Africa
Three cities—Tripoli
Victorious—Cairo
New flower—Addis Ababa
The place of cool waters—Nairobi
End of an elephant's trunk—Khartoum

Asia
Muddy confluence—Kuala Lumpur
Modern—Tehran
Garden—Riyadh
Anchor—Ankara
Father of a gazelle—Abu Dhabi

The Americas
Good winds—Buenos Aires
I saw a mountain—Montevideo
Peace—La Paz
Place of many fish—Panama
Traders—Ottawa

And for those familiar with London, can you guess the Tube Station from its origin?

Forge
Horse pond
Beer gate
Lace collar
Skin farm
Road to Ecgi's weir
Padda's farm
Dominican monks
Stream in a sacred wood
Sacred place that welcomes strangers

Forge—Hammersmith
Horse pond—Bayswater
Beer gate—Aldgate (ale gate)
Lace collar—Piccadilly
Skin farm—Hyde Park
Road to Ecgi's weir—Edgware Road
Padda's farm—Paddington
Dominican monks—Blackfriars
Stream in a sacred wood—Waterloo
Sacred place that welcomes strangers—Walthamstow

And finally, some multiple choice. What is the true derivation of each of these words?

Clue
a) A ball of yarn
b) A skeleton key
c) A love letter

Karaoke
a) Japanese for singing under water
b) Japanese for *howling*
c) Japanese for *empty orchestra*

Slogan
a) An Algonquian prayer
b) A Celtic war-cry
c) Russian for *repetition*

Boudoir

a) French for *sulking room*

b) French for *gun room*

c) French for *Peeping Tom*

Grocer

a) One who buys in gross

b) One who grows his own

c) One who is grossly fat

Hotbed

a) A medieval form of torture

b) A Victorian medical treatment

c) A covered flowerbed

Bollard

a) Tree trunk

b) Cricket ball

c) Dr. Cornelius Bollard

Kiosk

a) Aztec word for *umbrella*

b) Turkish word for *palace*

c) Burmese word for *hut*

Quarantine

a) Forty days

b) Asking time

c) Pseudo-prison

Bigot
a) Old English for *By God*
b) Old French for *thorn*
c) Old German for *stone wall*

Thesaurus
a) A riddling lizard from Greek mythology
b) A treasure chest
c) The book of Theseus

Beetle
a) Little biter
b) Little bean
c) Little bee

Aardvark
a) Swahili for *grandmother*
b) Dutch for *earth pig*
c) Croatian for *Jesus*

Pundit
a) Hindi for *wise man*
b) Irish for *counsellor*
c) Eskimo god of riddles

Winging it
a) Flying when the engine has failed
b) Eating only the chicken wings (and not the breast)
c) An actor learning his lines in the wings

Quiz
a) Latin for *who is?*
b) Hindi for *unclaimed property*
c) Chinese for *escape*

The answers:

Clue
a) A ball of yarn

Karaoke
c) Japanese for *empty orchestra*

Slogan
b) A Celtic war-cry

Boudoir
a) French for *sulking room*

Grocer
a) One who buys in gross

Hotbed
c) A covered flowerbed

Bollard
a) Tree trunk

Kiosk
b) Turkish word for *palace*

Quarantine
a) Forty days

Bigot
a) Old English for *By God*

Thesaurus
b) A treasure chest

Beetle
a) Little biter

Aardvark
b) Dutch for *earth pig*

Pundit
a) Hindi for *wise man*

Winging it
c) An actor learning his lines in the wings

Quiz
a) Latin for *who is?*

THE CREAM OF
THE SOURCES

A book like this would need a bibliography at least twice its own size; so in the interest of paper preservation, there isn't one.

I can, though, assure you that everything in here has been checked, mainly against the following works:

The Oxford English Dictionary
The Oxford Dictionary of Place Names
The Oxford Dictionary of English Surnames (Reany & Wilson)
The Dictionary of Idioms by Linda and Roger Flavell
The Dictionary of National Biography
Brewer's Dictionary of Phrase and Fable

And online:

The Online Etymology Dictionary
Phrases.org

And (with vast circumspection):

Dear old Wikipedia (or *Fastchild*)

Unfortunately, there are many points on which these sources disagree. Usually, rather than take you carefully through all of the arguments and counter-arguments, I have simply picked the one that I believe is most likely and recounted that.

All other things being equal, I have trusted them in the order in which they are listed above. However, if a good citation is produced then I am quite prepared to side with the underdog.

Occasionally, I've given citations that you won't find in any work of reference because I've found them all by myself. So for confused scholars who suspect me of making things up as I go along:

"Draw a blank": *The History of Great Britain*, Arthur Wilson (1643)

"Blank cheque": *An Inquiry into the Various Systems of Political Economy*, Charles Ganilh (1812)

"Talk cold turkey": *One of Three*, Clifford Raymond (1919)

"Crap" and "Number one": *Poems in Two Volumes*, J. Churchill Esq. (1801)

"Dr. Placebo": *Bath Memoirs*, Robert Pierce (1697), quoted in *Attempts to Revive Antient Medical Doctrines*, Alexander Sutherland (1763) and elsewhere

"Pass the buck": *The Conquest of Kansas*, William Phillips (1856)